denver overnight

aj morocco

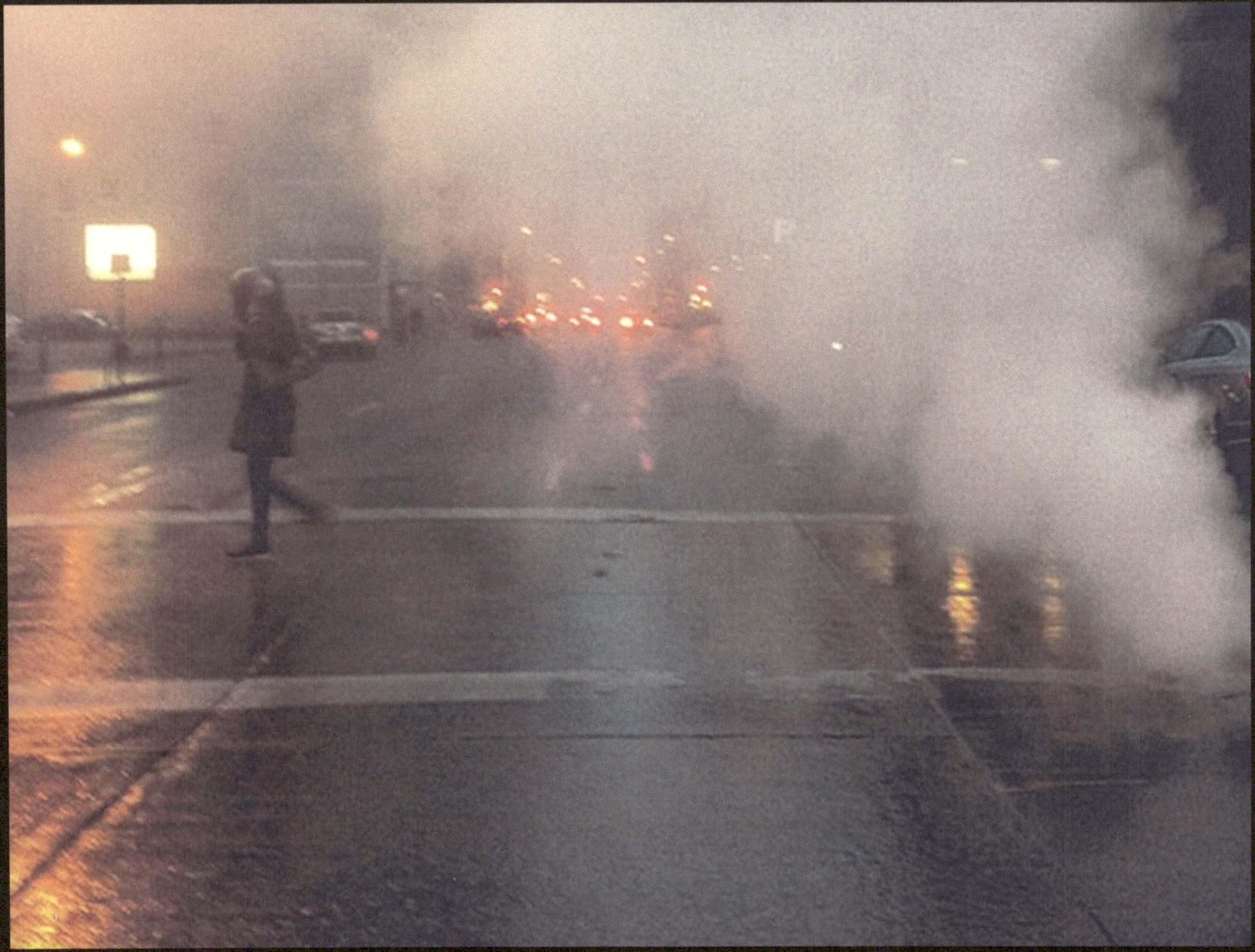

Published in the United States by Koebner Triangle Press; Denver, CO

First Printing

ISBN: 978-0-9895824-9-0

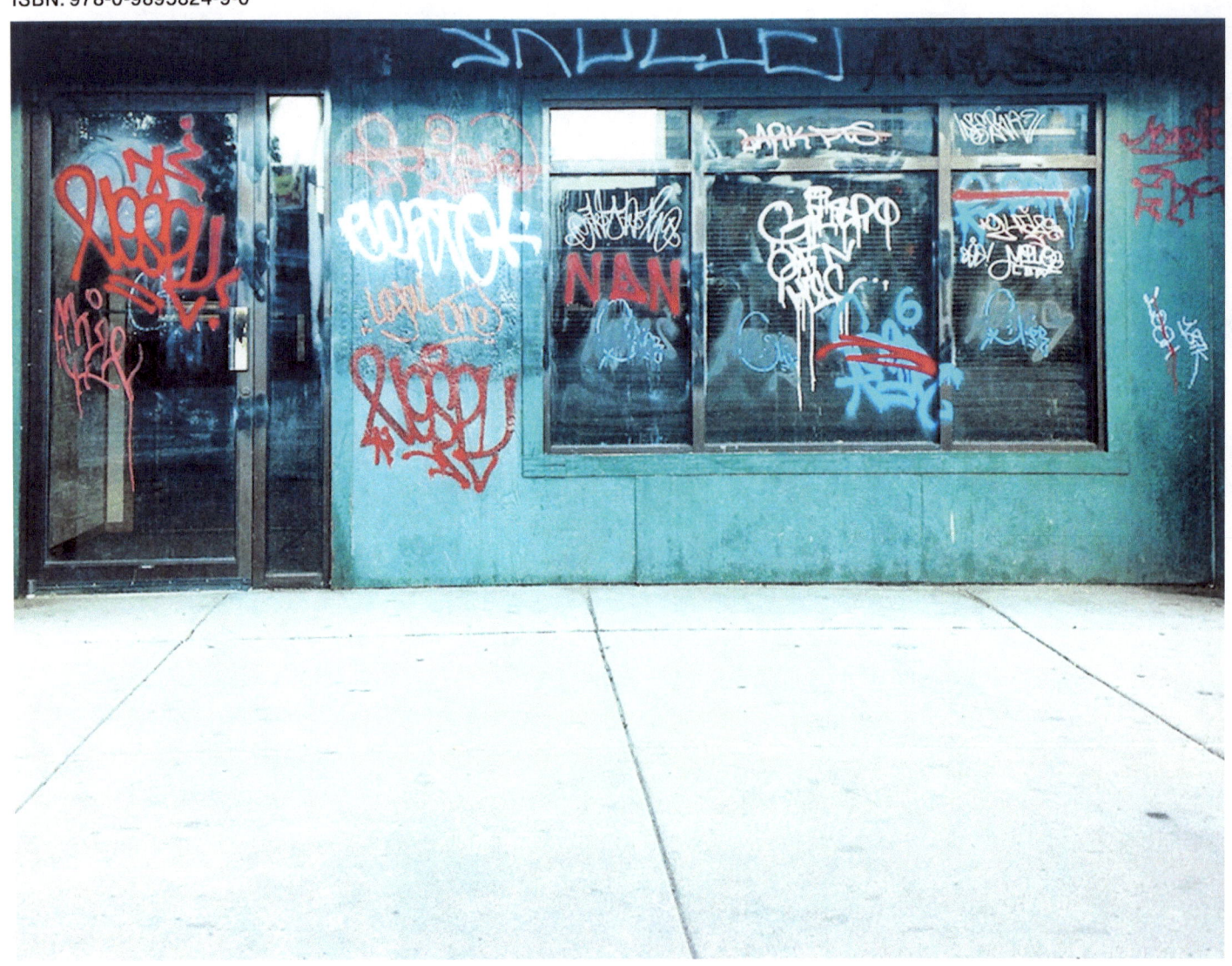

2075 North Broadway

denver overnight

aj morocco

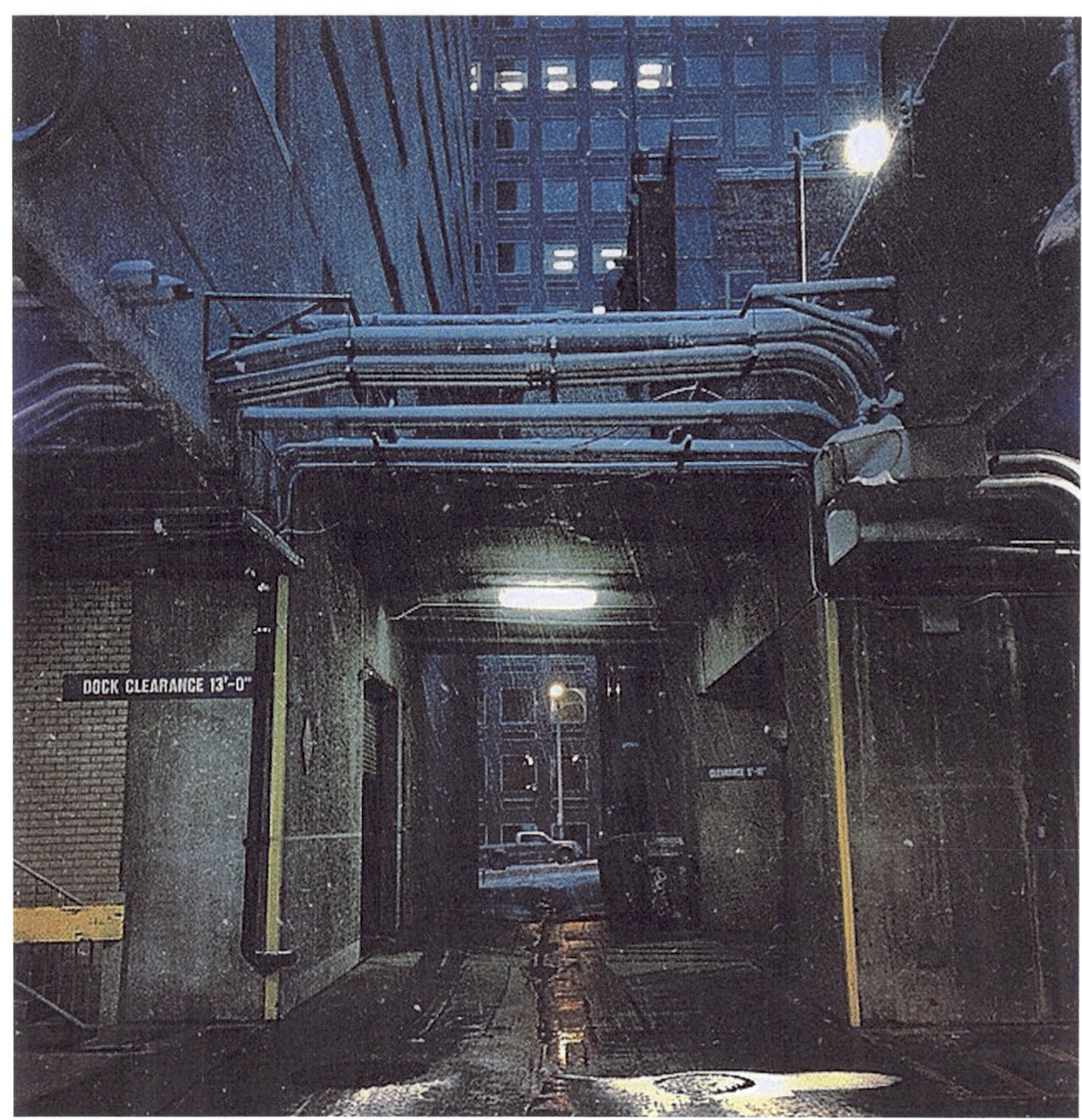

Alley off East 17th between Lincoln & Sherman

dedication

to my Mom, Frances Benish, who gave me a Kodak 4000 Disc camera when I was 11

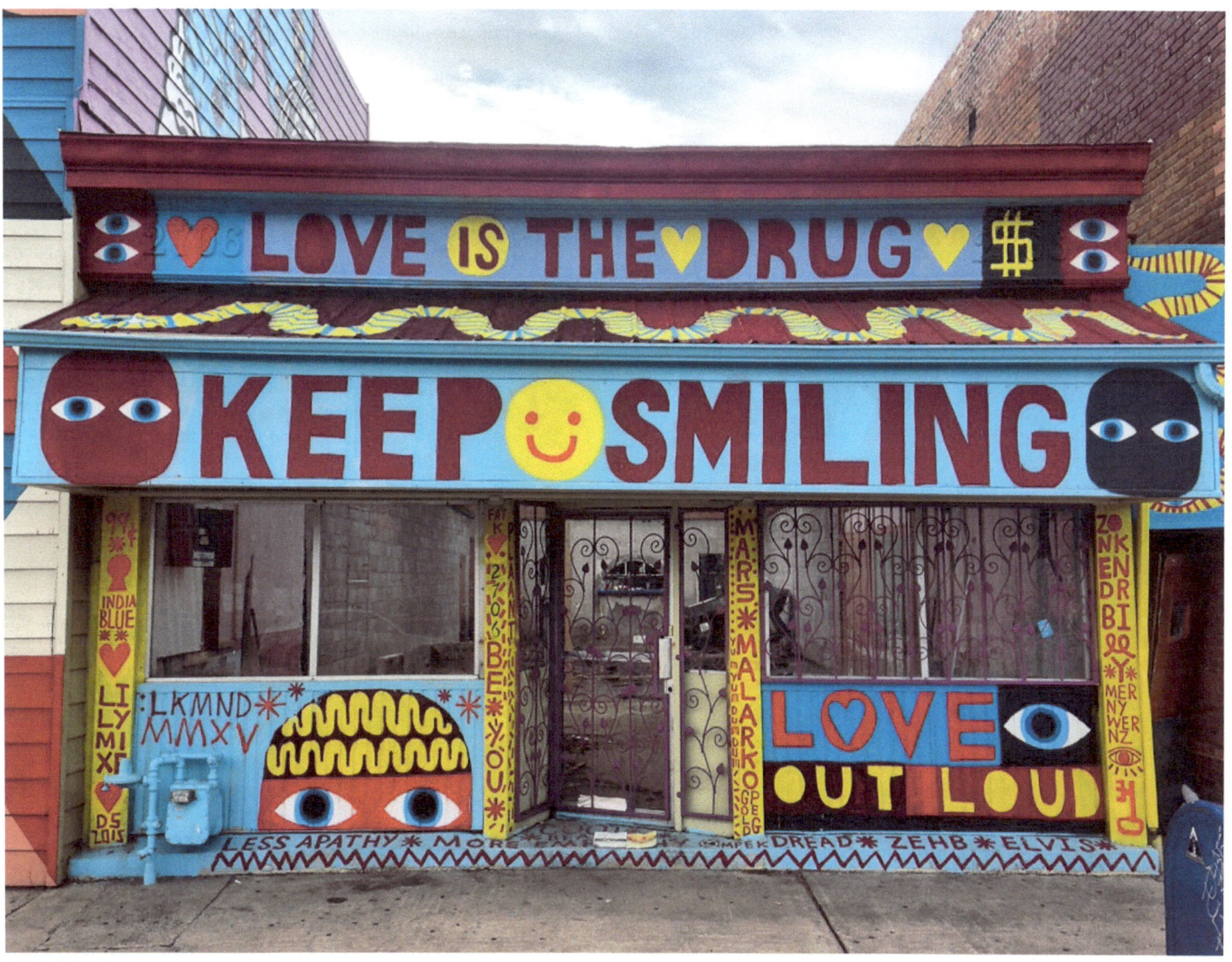

2706 Larimer

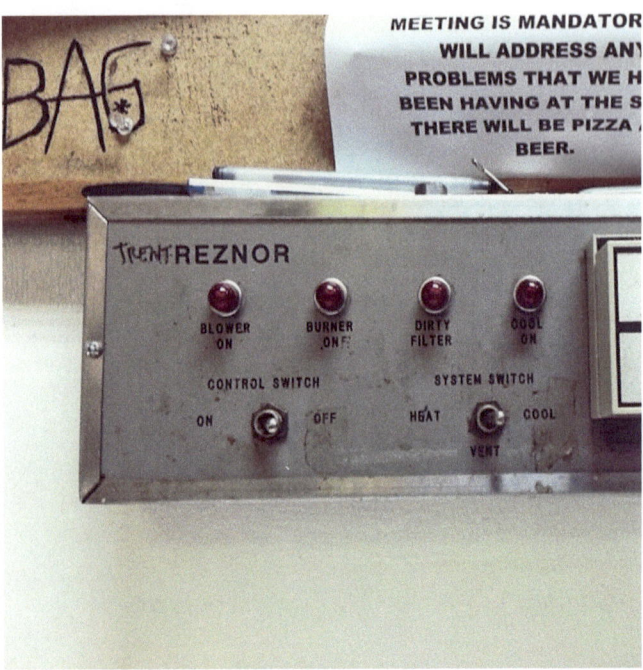

good morning, midnight

It all started with the accident in November 2012. A tractor-trailer totaled my Subaru on northbound I-25, between Denver and Fort Collins, Colorado. The car was a goner, which was a bummer because I was one payment away from finally owning the damn thing and had just installed a new stereo. Luckily, I wasn't a goner — somehow I had walked away from the accident, but barely.

Weeks and months went by. After watching every movie in our house and eating enough grilled cheese sandwiches to stack up to the moon, I got off my ass and started exercising and doing yoga. By the spring of 2013, I was doing better and could at least move around with relative ease. During the whole time I was down and out, I had no job and no income except for eBay, so I had to start somewhere.

My wife gently prodded me to put on pants and update my resume. Honestly, she was right. It was overdue. I hadn't done anything for what seemed like a year, and had nothing to add to my resume to account for my recovery time or lack of ambition I was feeling at the time.

Around that same time, my friend Kim needed help at a restaurant she was managing. She needed someone to deliver the commercial food orders for their wholesale fresh-baked bagels, all over Denver. She explained the trouble with the job was the hours: start at 3 a.m., done by 7 a.m. By sheer luck or coincidence, this lined up perfectly with my schedule. I could get home by 7:30 a.m., right as my wife was leaving for work. She would literally hand over our infant daughter as we passed by one another each morning. The arrangement at least let us save on childcare costs.

The hours didn't bother me. In fact, I kinda liked the idea of working when everyone was sleeping. I had worked overnight before. After high school, I briefly worked the 10 p.m. to 6 a.m. shift at a gas station back home in New Jersey. Another time, I worked as a night shift cashier for six grueling months at a convenience store in Boston in the Back Bay neighborhood. I don't want to mince words here. It stinks staying up all night and going to bed with birds chirping. It sucks being awake and alone on your days off. Everybody else out there, living in the sunlight, going to parks and cookouts and gyms and cozy day jobs… And there you are. Sleeping the day away like a lazy vampire. Working overnight changes you and it's not healthy for your body or mind. It's not good money either, but what is these days?

There was one aspect to the gig that made it different from all those other jobs I slogged through as an adolescent. With those jobs, I stood still in one place and couldn't leave. This job was the opposite. Kim needed me to be out there, constantly moving around, delivering to hotels and restaurants all over the city. I took the job and started that weekend.

Before the bagel delivery job, I would have to admit I only kinda sorta knew my way around Denver. I hadn't taken the time to learn the streets, and often relied on GPS or friends to direct me despite living in the city for several years. After about a month, I could visually tell the difference between 15th and 18th streets, could name landmarks, and actually give directions to help others. The job was a crash course in Denver geography, so I quickly learned the city upside-down and backwards.

Denver, a major American city, does not have an "overnight culture" the way it's contemporary costal cities do. We don't have many 24-hour enterprises other than the airport and most of our all-night commercial ventures are food industry related. There's a lot of food production, prep, distribution and packaging done at 4 in the morning here in Denver.

Most of these businesses aren't open to the public, so the larger working-class, overnight culture is rarely seen or heard by the average person. When you work overnight, it's like reverse banker's hours. It gets light out instead of getting dark out. People rush in to work while you leisurely take your time, heading home in the opposite direction (with the sun not glaring into your eyes), smile on your face because you don't have to deal with traffic or meetings.

Working when everyone is asleep can be surreal sometimes. It can get eerily quiet. During bad weather, it can seem downright apocalyptic. The best time to see Denver overnight is during a snowstorm, when everyone is watching TV in their jammies. The city is much different without traffic, without scooters, without the oppressive summer heat, without the people. I experienced serene moments of beauty in this city… at 4:50 a.m. when no one else was around. So, I started taking pictures of those moments. Night photography became a productive, healthy way to remain sane and kill time between my deliveries — provided I didn't get hit by a car or mugged or anything like that. I had a lot of time to burn. For example, I might have to wait for a coffee shop manager to show up and had twenty minutes to kill. That time could be spent sitting safety in my warm car, or it could be spent by walking around exploring.

I drove and walked all over the city — on every street, every alley, every accessible rooftop, every neighborhood. I've been inside every skyscraper (even the secure ones) and office complexes. I've been inside the D&F Tower, the top of the Republic Plaza, inside the U.S. Mint, the Capital, backstage at the Pepsi Center, the players' entrance to Coors Field, and every bar and diner from here to Aurora. Probably.

After a year had gone by, I pushed myself even further and started trying to get into obscure or hidden places: private alleys, light rail tunnels, hidden gardens, abandoned buildings, a private speakeasy. I got into all kinds of places but never got into trouble — I was there to take photos and not to steal or be malicious.

I discovered that taking photos at night is way harder than it looks. There are so many obstacles to contend with. So many things can go wrong. First and foremost on that list of problems is that during the winter, some mornings were so cold that my camera wouldn't function properly. Other times I'd have to walk a quarter mile in the snow or endure stinging rain just because the lighting was right. This part time hobby challenged me and kept my mind sharp, even though it was exhausting. I took photos of things that interested me:

handwritten signs, graffiti murals, vintage mannequins, telephone pole wheat pastings, mailboxes, mossy bricks, old cars, light rail tunnels and neurotic baseball fans.

Professional photographers spend years developing their style. They study the technical and mechanical aspects of photography like aperture settings, using proper lenses, perfecting the manual settings. For me, this experiment focused on the other side of the coin — being in the right place at the right time. I am not a pro in any sense of the word. There's nothing technical about that whatsoever. My goal wasn't to produce the sharpest image with the highest resolution or to frame the perfect shot. It was more about capturing unscripted moments, studying the ephemeral that we normally walk past.

I used a vintage Nikon film camera and a digital Cannon EOS Rebel, but I mainly used an old iPhone for most of my photos. You can't exactly walk around with expensive camera equipment and set up a tripod in the middle of the street, even at 3:45 a.m. It attracts unwanted attention and that's the last thing you want to deal with. I learned to be covert about it, never announcing my presence or intentions.

I've already outlined that the hours I worked were early morning, yet invariably, someone glancing through my photos always points out, "that picture was taken in the daylight," or something like that. As if I'm cheating on my own theme. Well, in my defense, there's daylight during that chunk of time. And, believe it or not, the sun often rises. It was not unusual for me to get my best photos right at, or immediately after, sunrise.

During the dead of night, from closing time to sunrise, is when you see the most interesting people and the strangest novelties. Yet, due to the lighting, it's very hard to capture these events. It's almost impossible to commit those fast moving, dark shadows to film, but this is my best effort to do so. I remembered the locations of about 90 percent of these photos, and tried my best to label addresses for them; although, I did leave out some at personal residences when necessary.

From spring 2013 to summer 2016, I took over 3,500 photos in the Denver metro area. I explored and documented the architecture, signs and people in my adopted city as I worked nights and battled insomnia and slowly recovered from the physical and mental trauma of a major car accident. This book collects some of my personal favorites and greatest hits from this project. Thanks for checking it out.

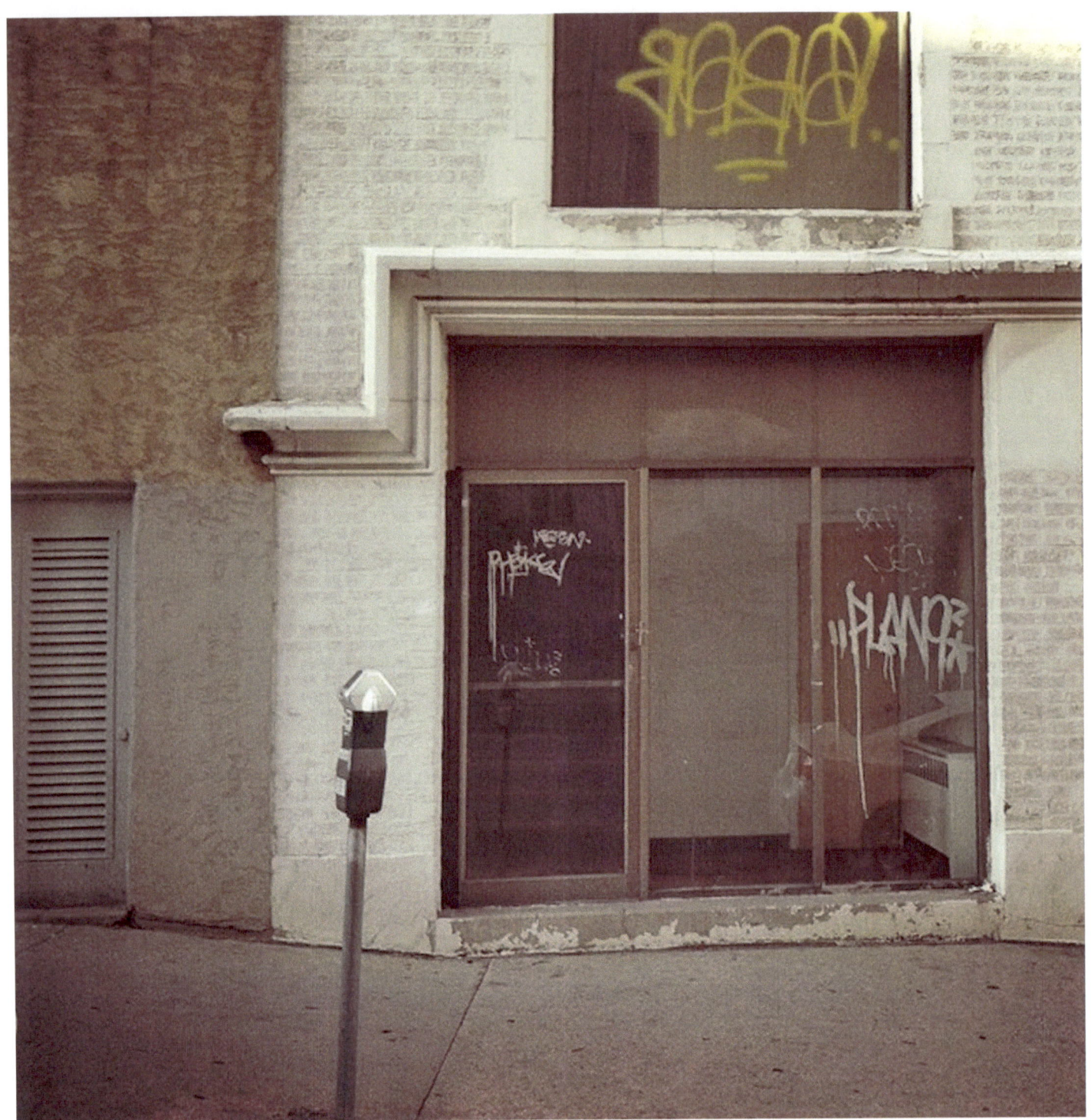

East 13th Avenue between Sherman & Lincoln

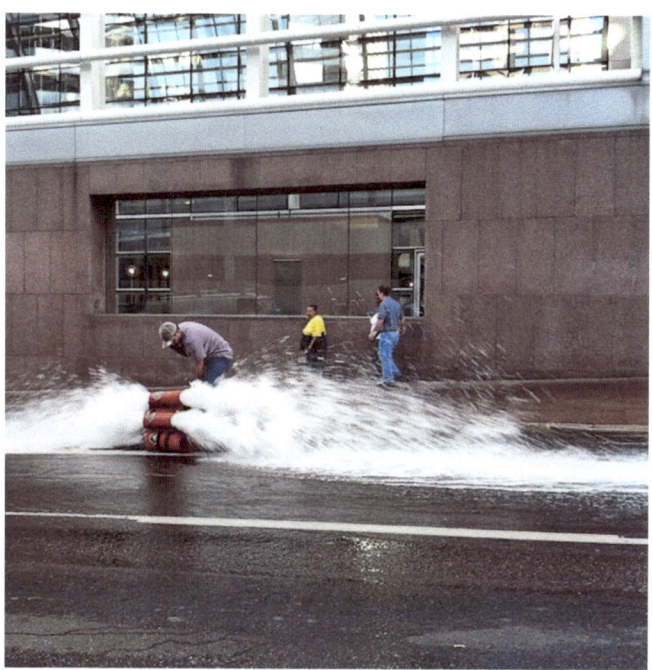

East 17th & Lincoln

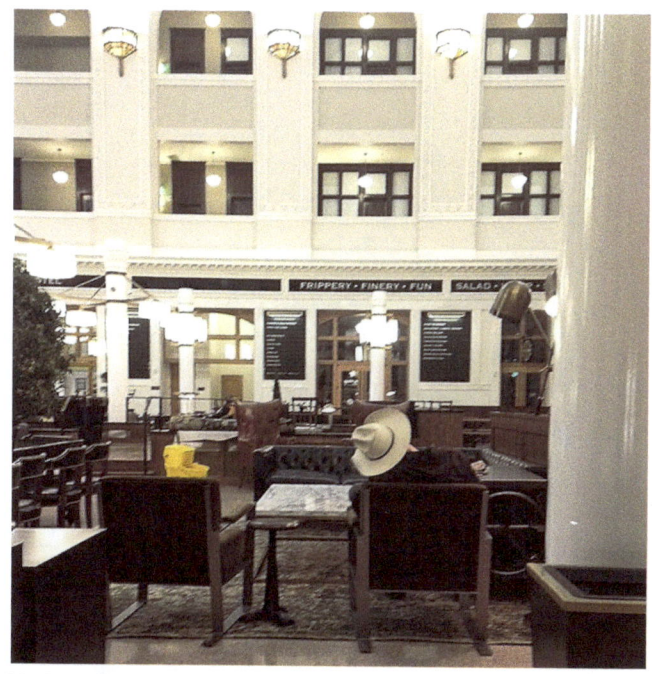

Union Station lounge

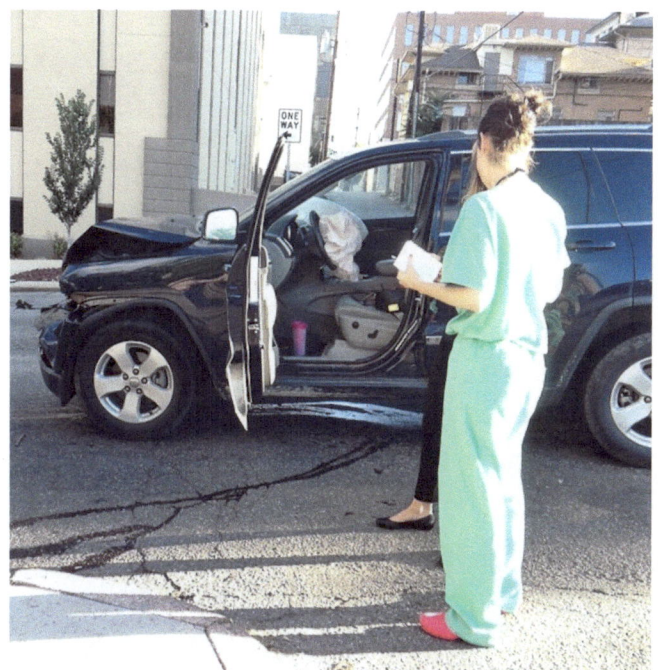

8th Avenue between Grant & Logan

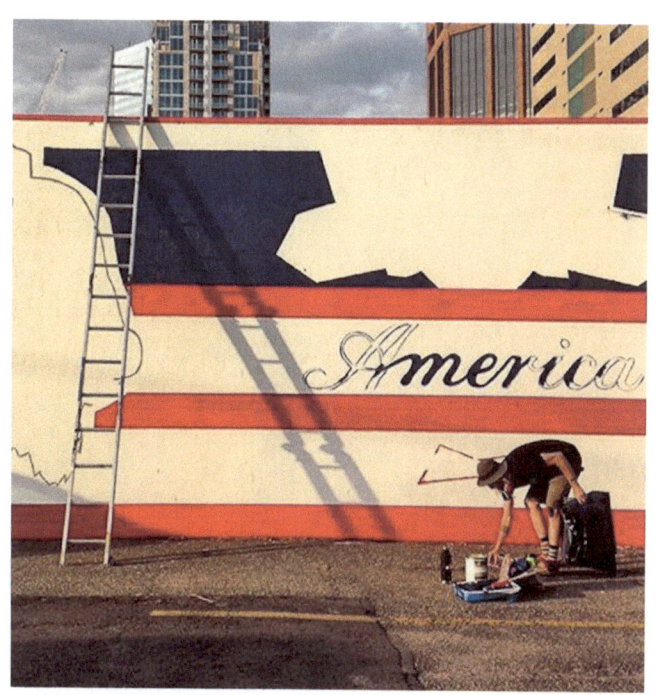

1900 North Broadway

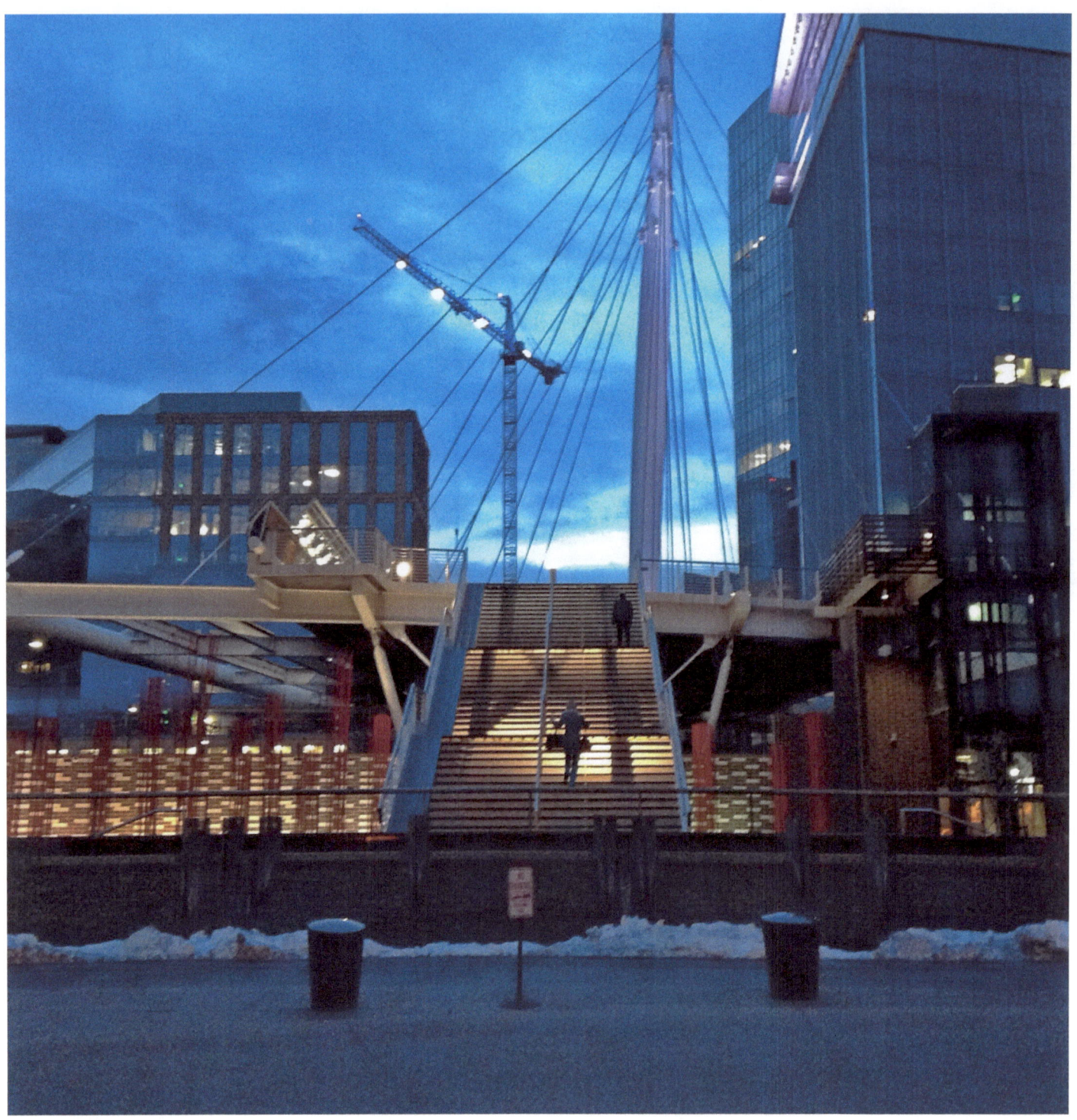

1602 Little Raven

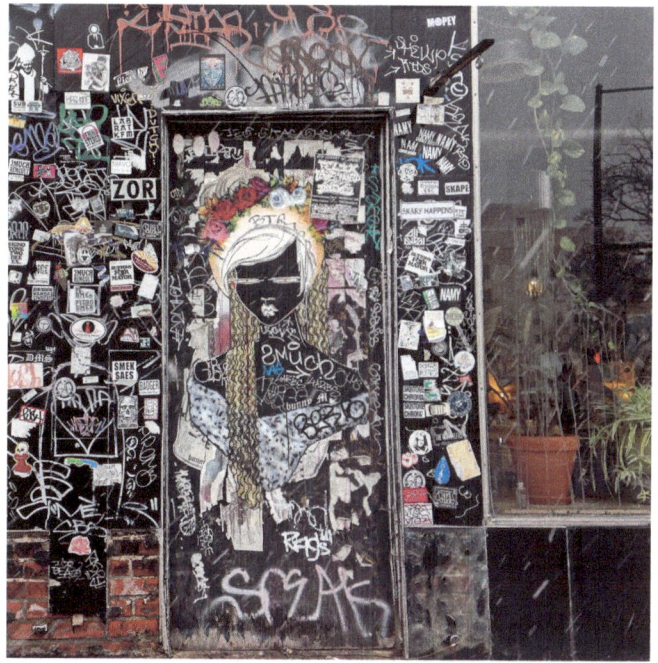

206 East 13th

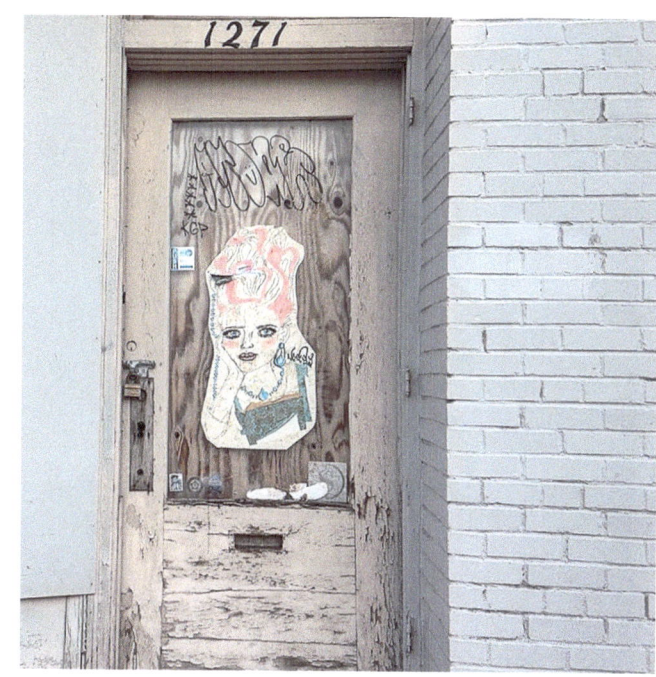

1271 Sherman

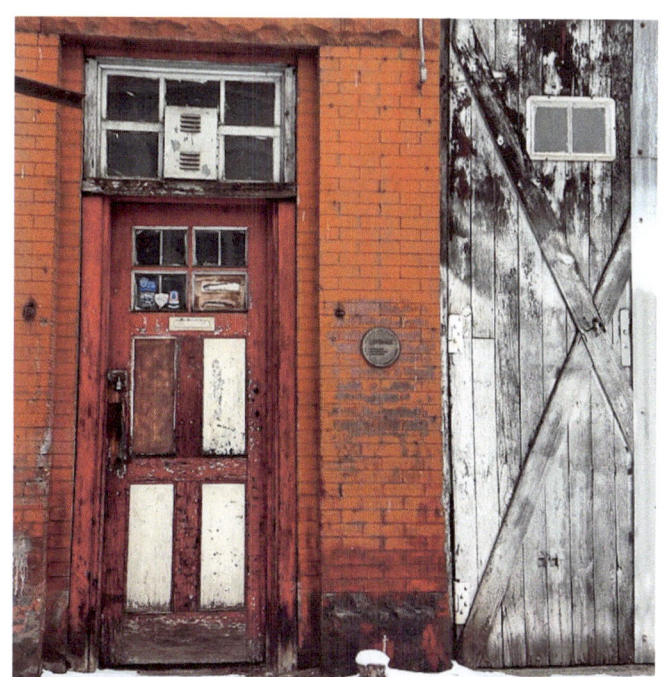

1999 Chesnut

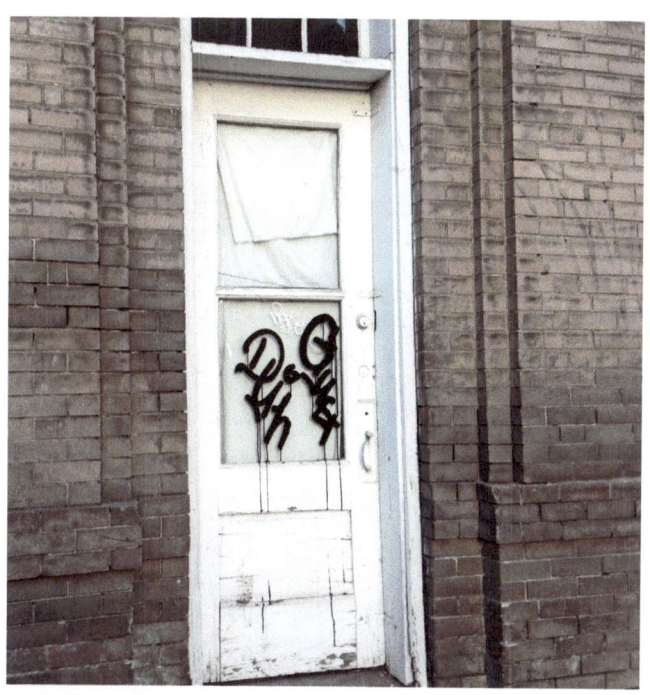

821 Corona

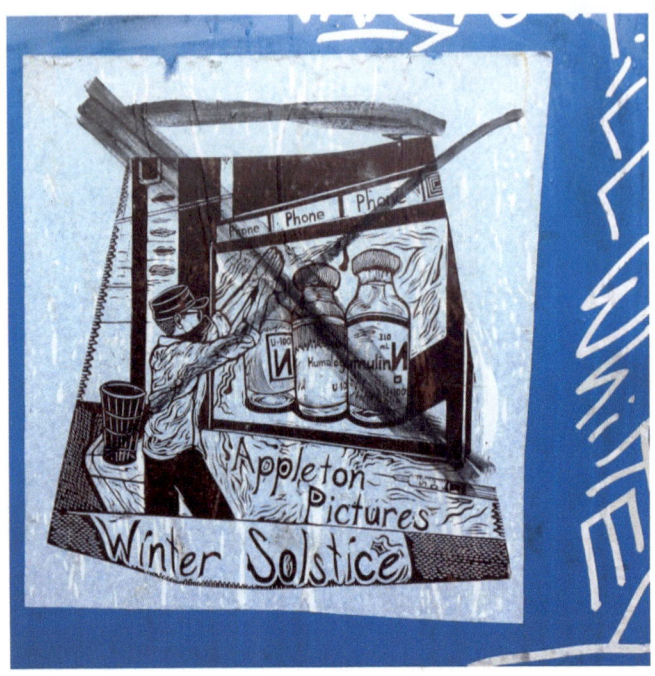

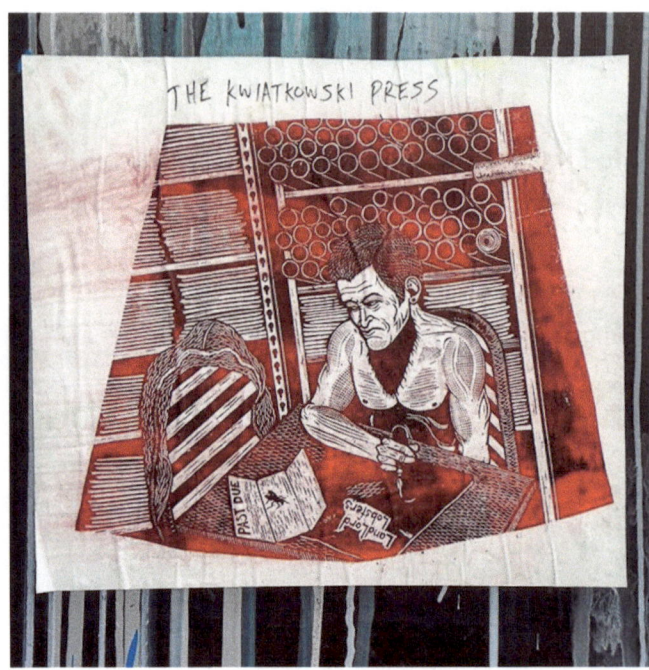

I documented thousands of pieces of street art in Denver. Murals, stickers, tags, throw ups, wild style flash, intricate line work, highbrow art and bad graffiti. My favorite of the regular locals is an outsider artist named Frank Kwiatkowski.

One day, I was up in the Five Points neighborhood very early in the morning when I saw this wheat pasting on an old telephone pole. Then I saw another. And another. The more I looked, the more I noticed The Kwiatkowki Press attached to dumpsters, utility poles, telecom junction boxes… they were all over the downtown area. Reoccurring themes seemed to be oozing from Frank's art. Diabetes and insulin. Celebrities. Being alone. Vandalism. Society.

Each morning I would look for these wheat pastings. It was like a mini scavenger hunt. Each wheat pasting featured a different print and accompanying text. Some were printed on the backs of giant recycled maps, old butcher block paper, or discarded architectural blueprints.

Frank kept my mind fresh and engaged, even though we never met. I was, and still am, a big fan of his work.

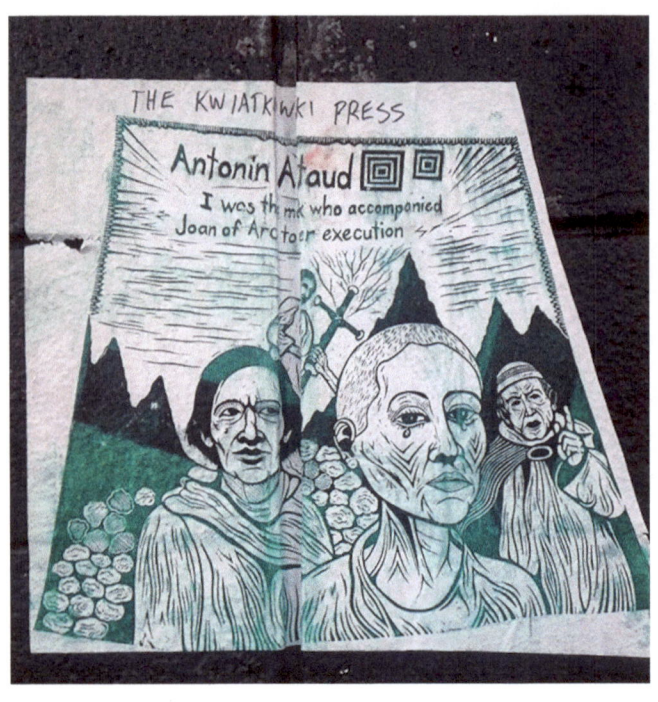

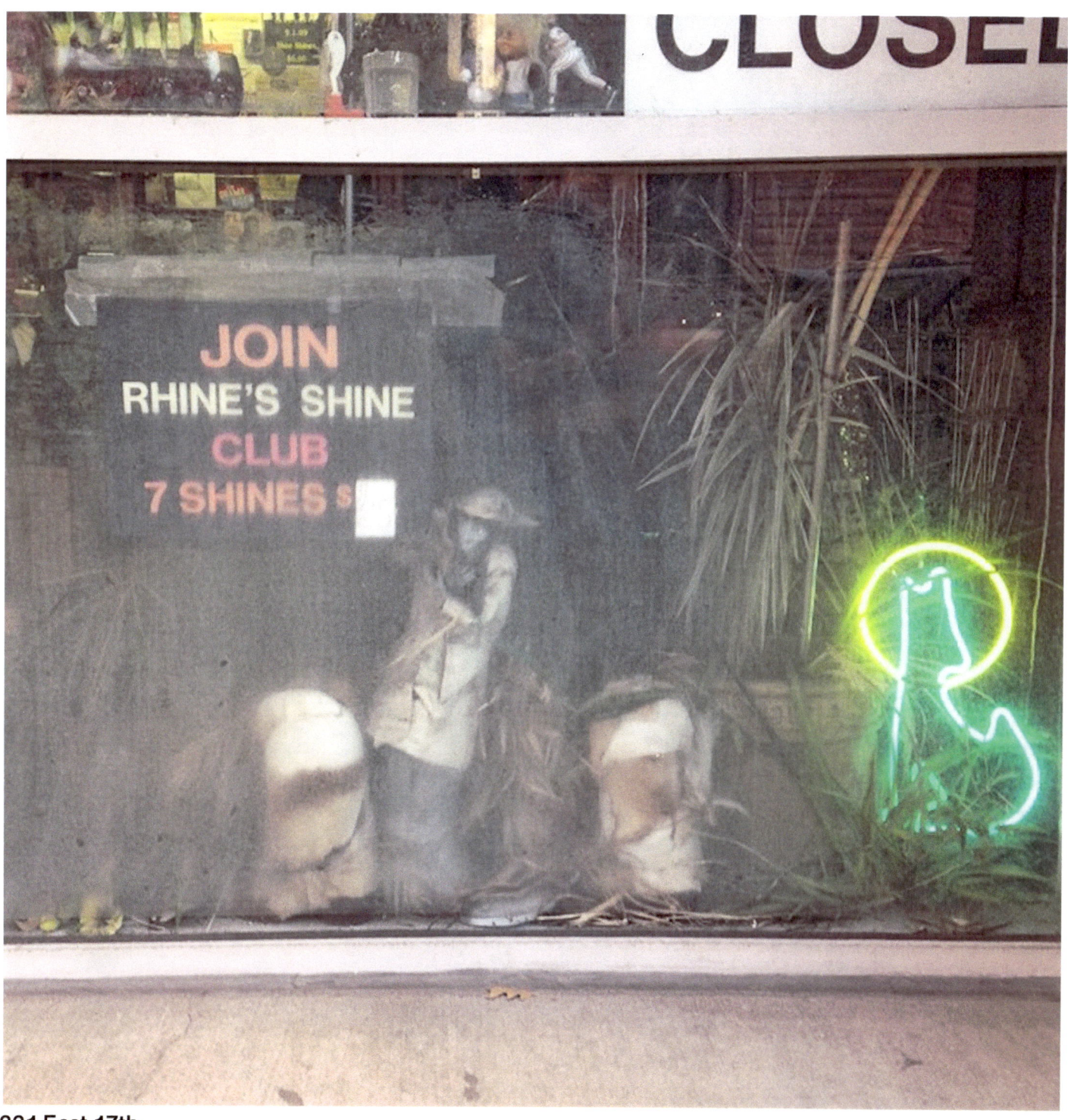

221 East 17th

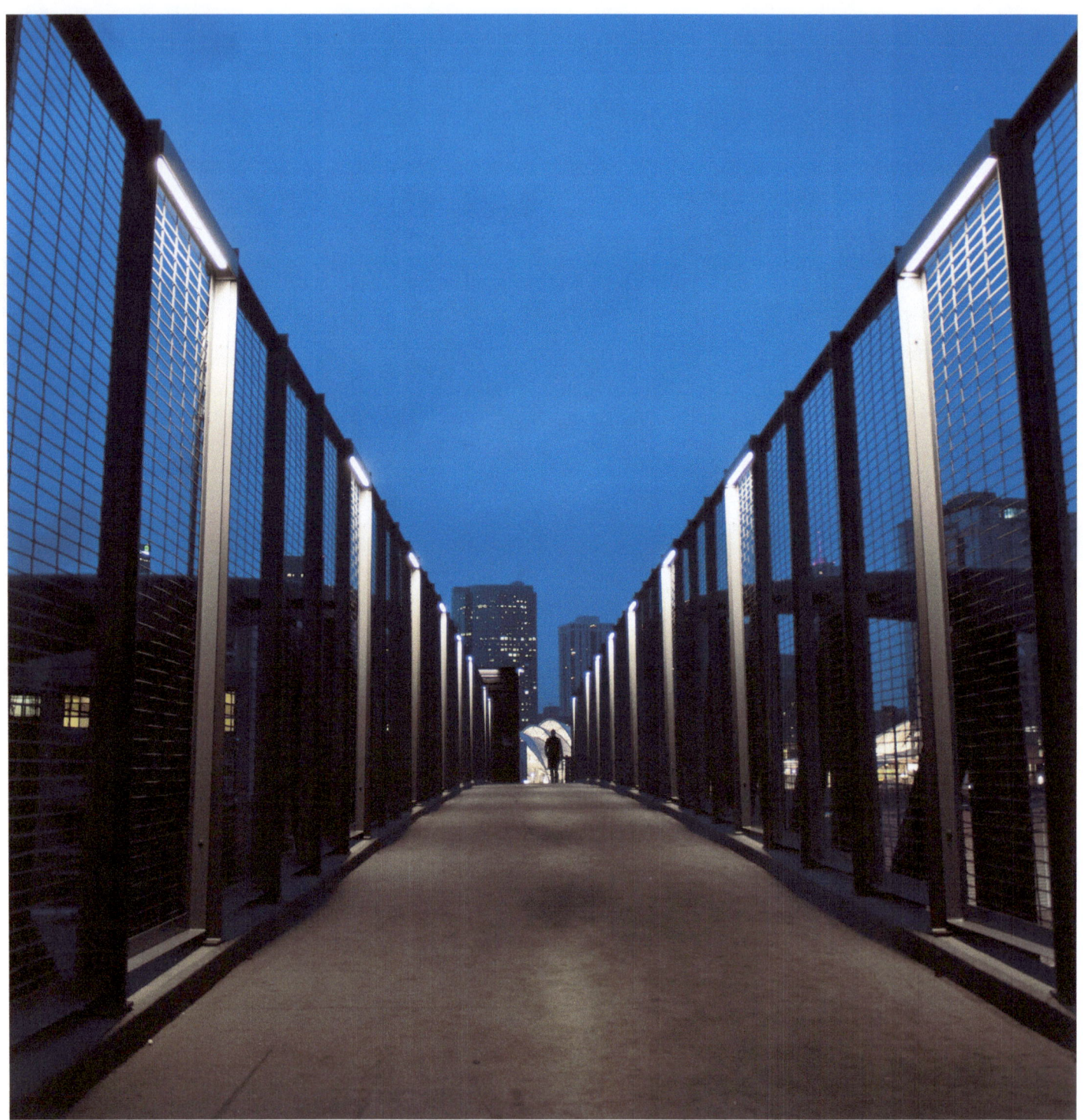

18th Street footbridge

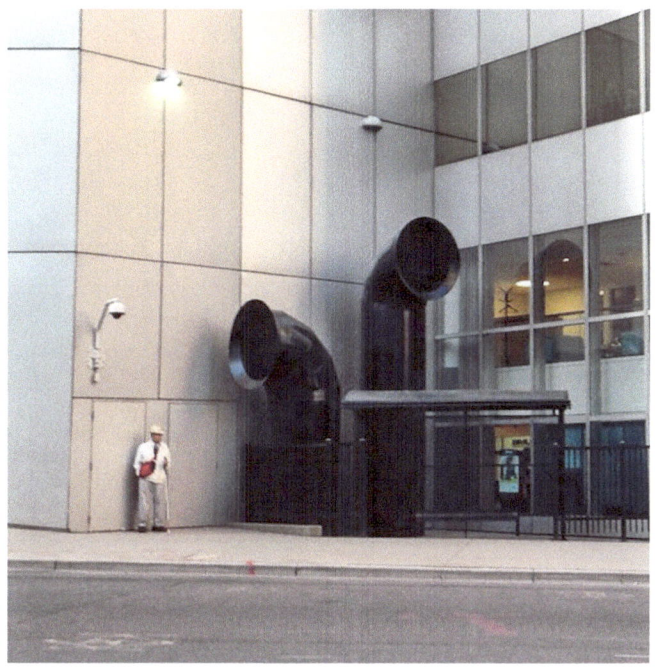

166 East 17th

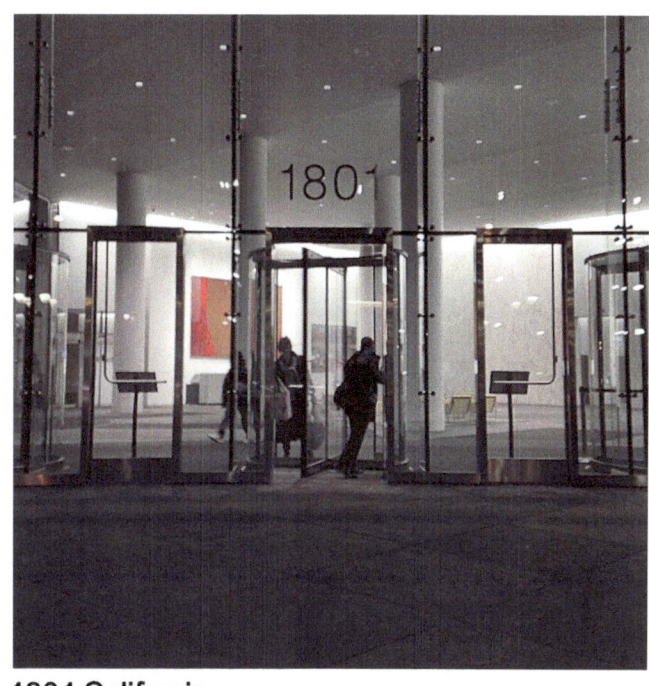

1801 California

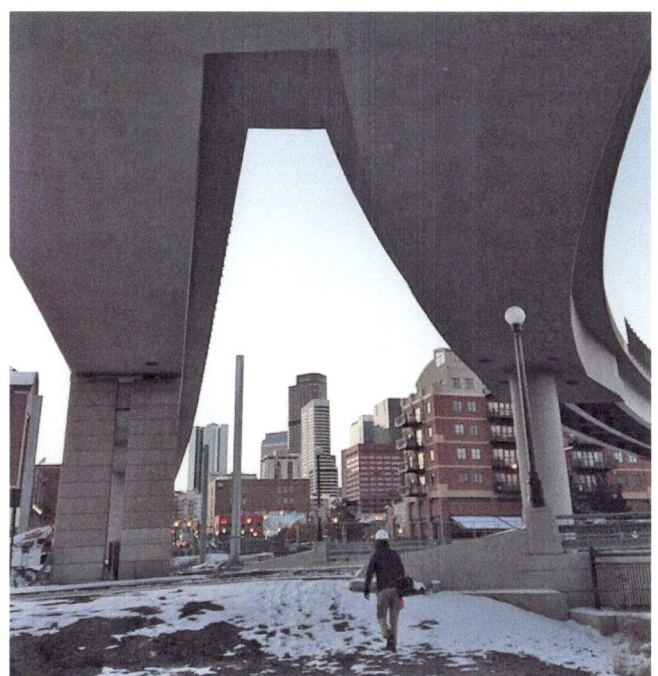

Wewatta Street underneath the I-25 ramps

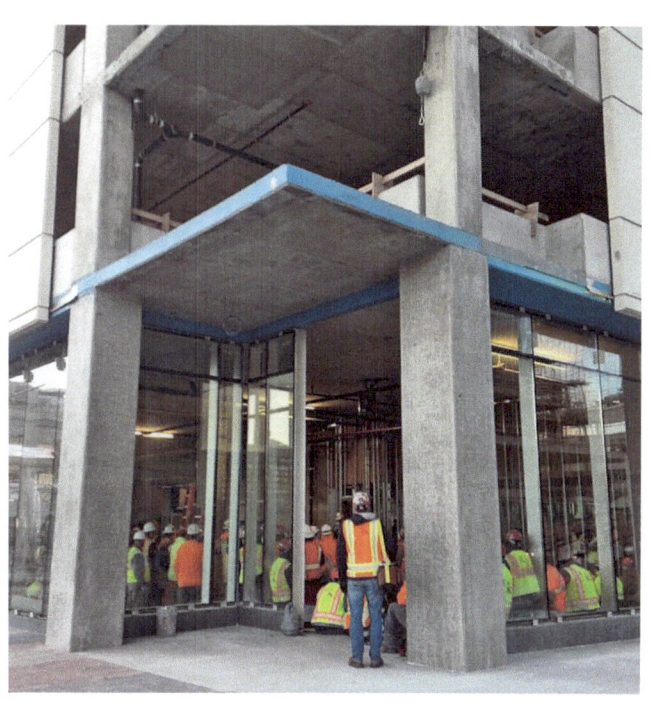

1650 Wewatta

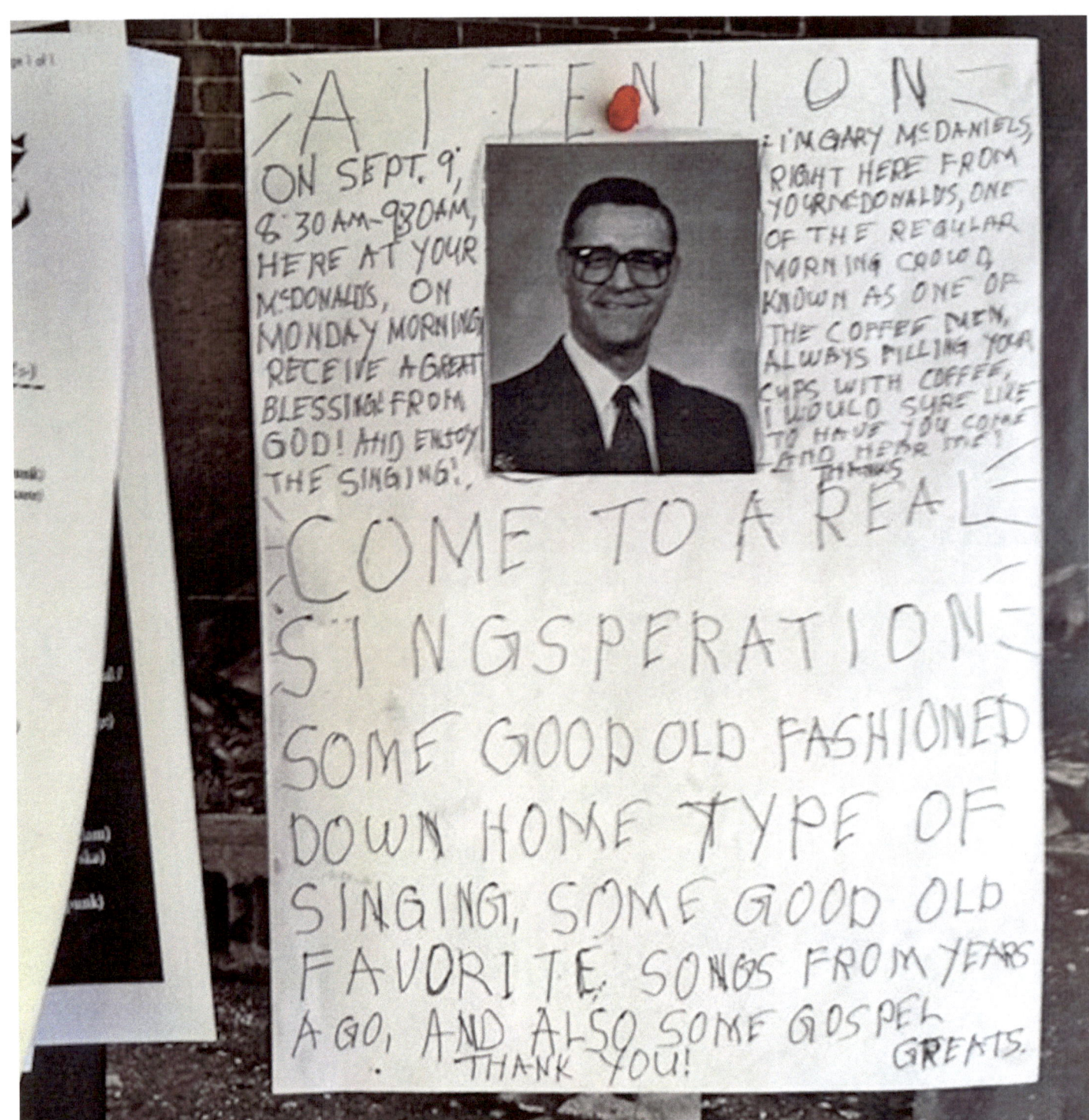

1350 West Colfax

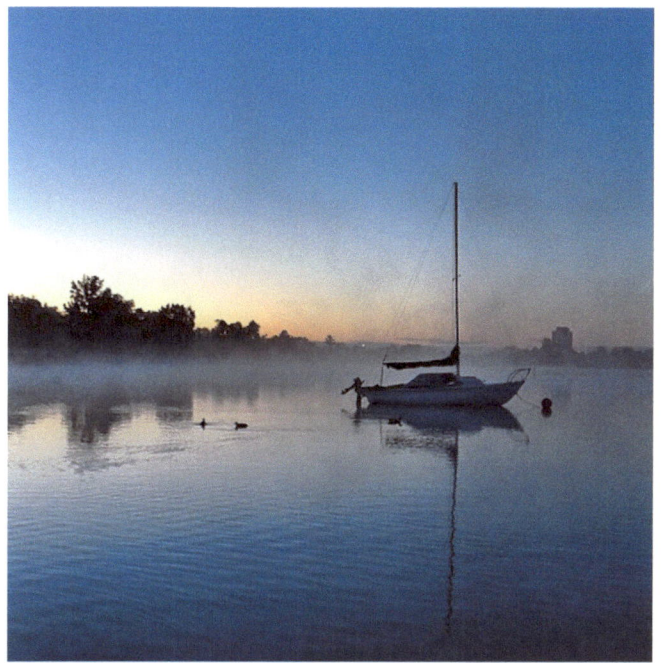

Sloan Lake

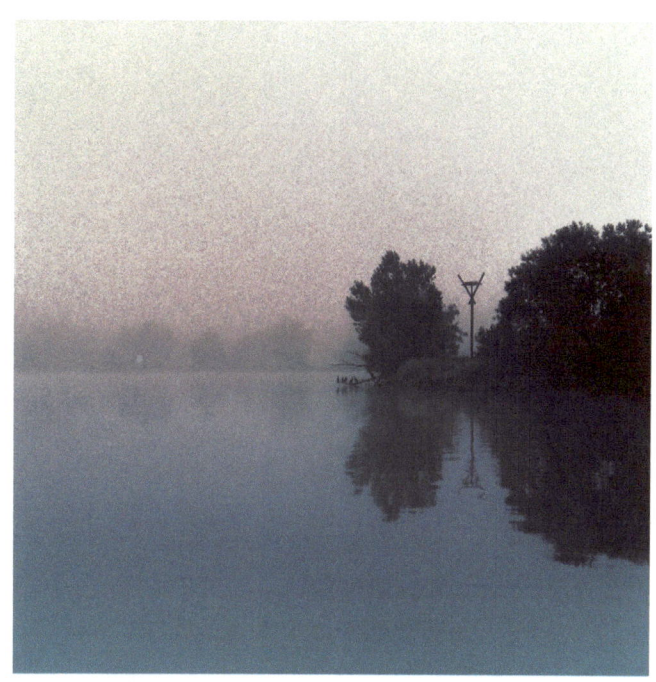

Sloan Lake

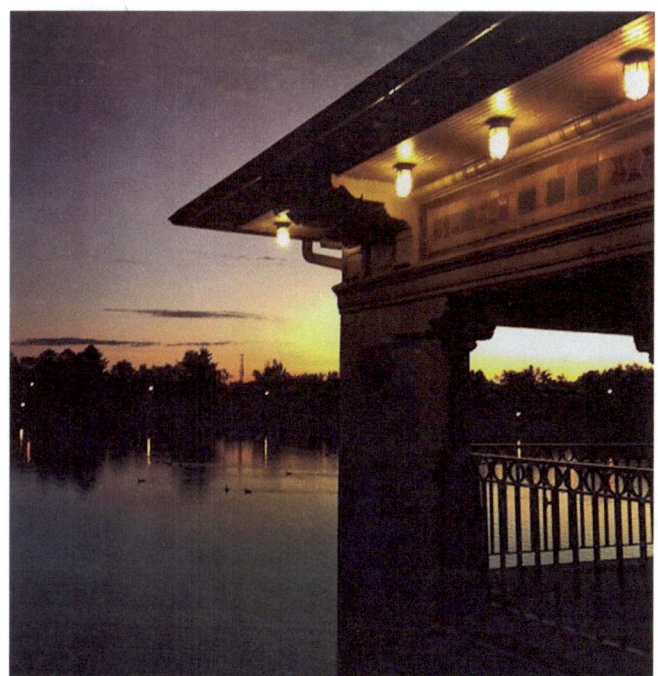

Smith Lake

Sloan Lake

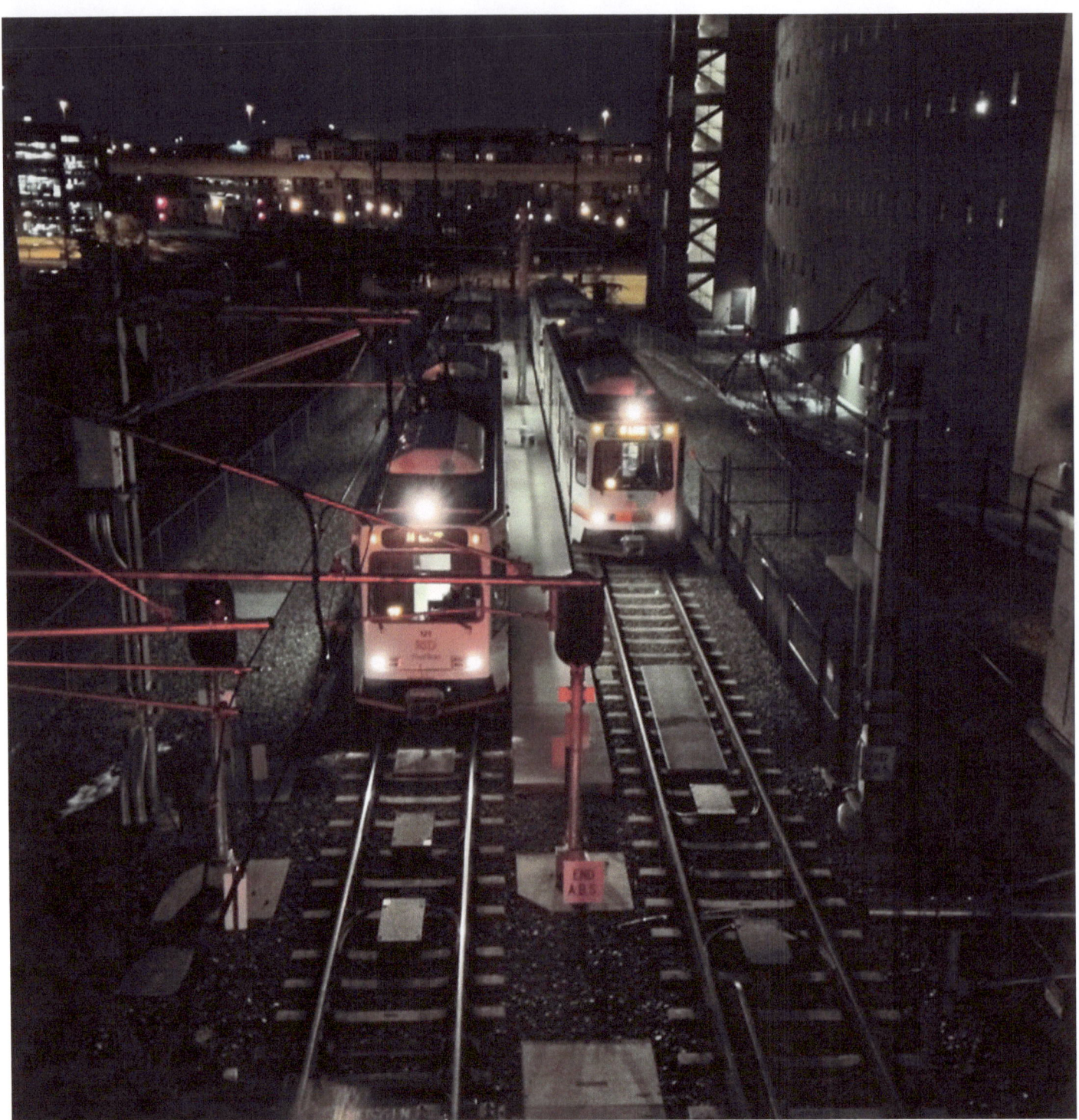

18th Street footbridge

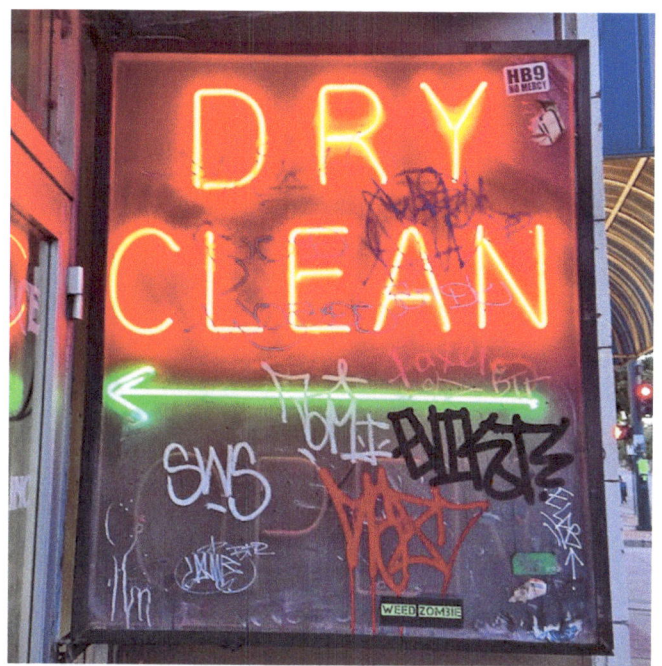

94 South Broadway

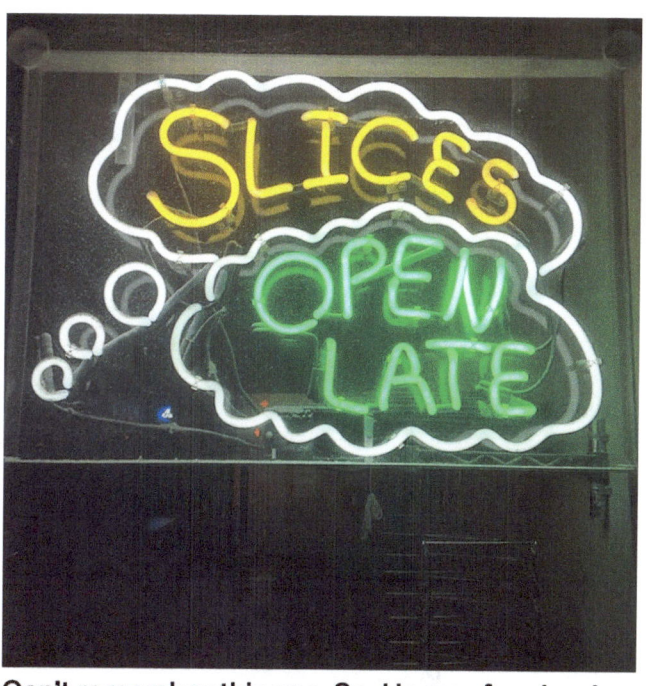

Can't remember this one. So. Hooray for pizza!

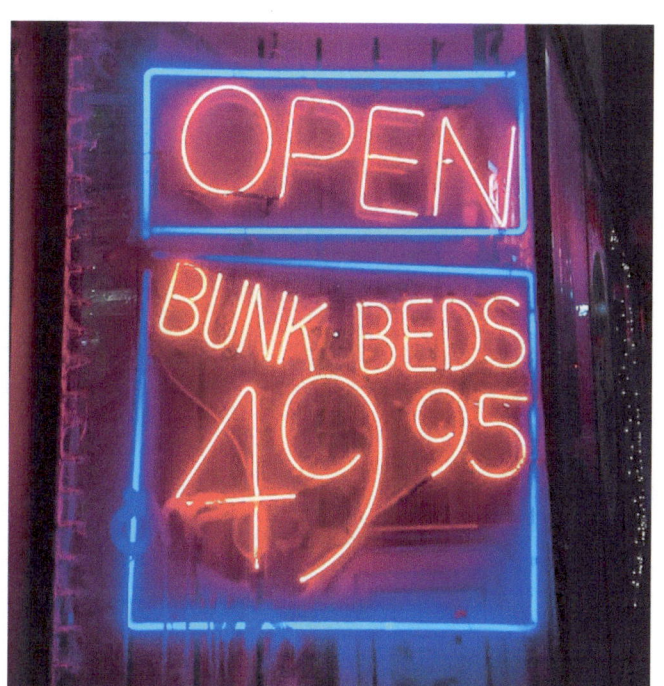

410 East Colfax

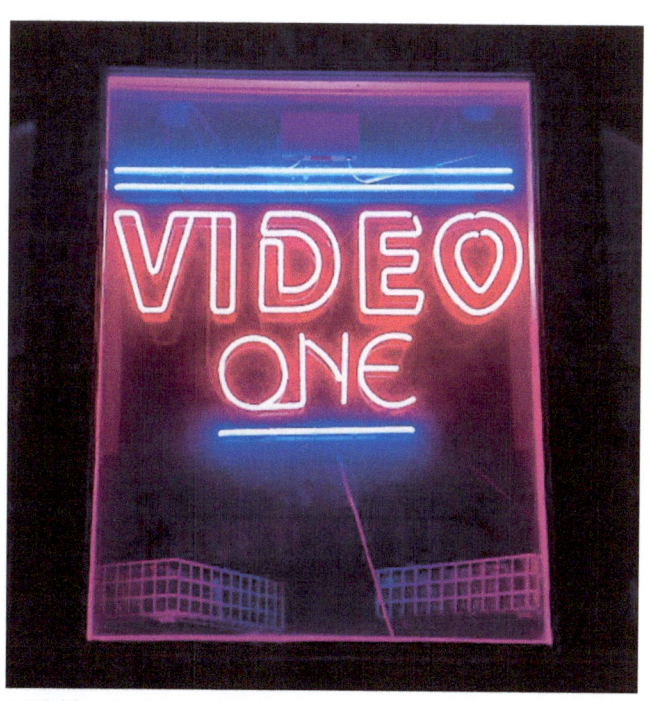

600 North Downing

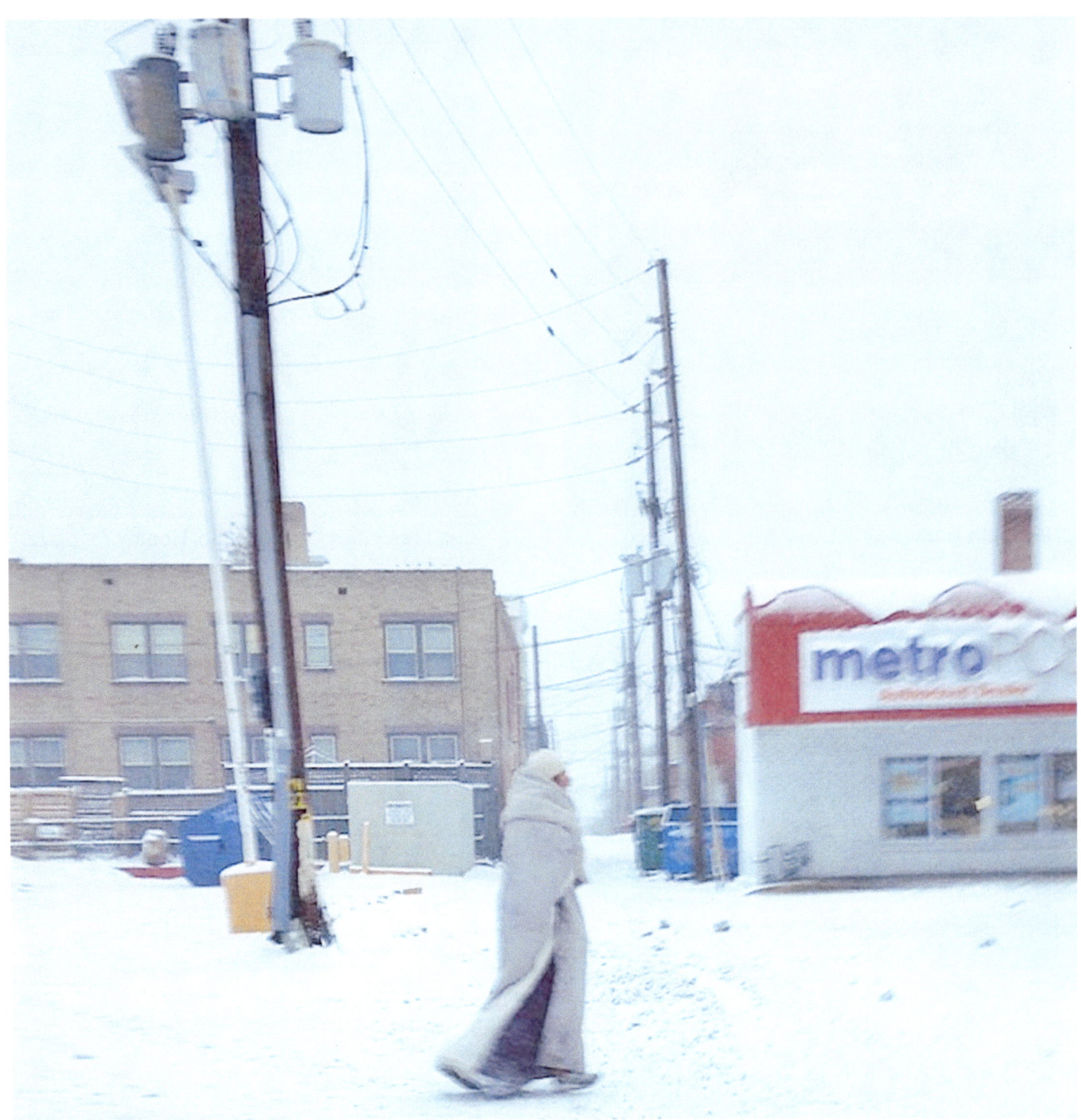

1121 East Colfax

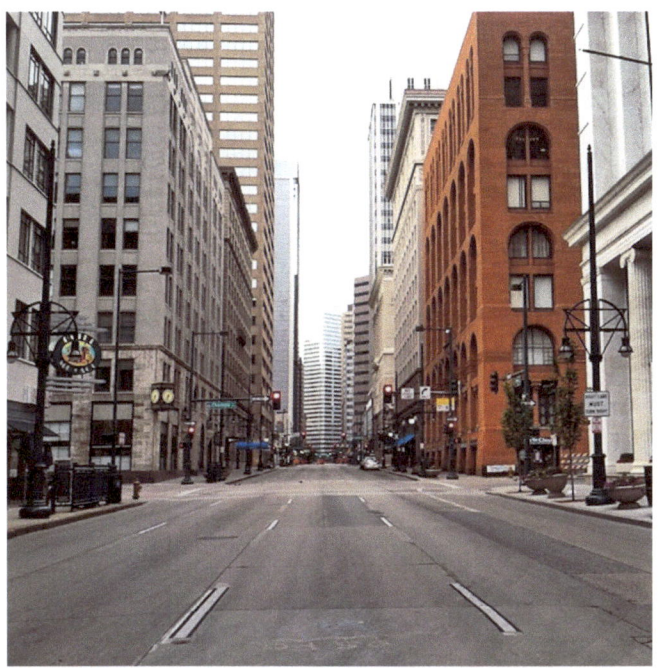

17th & Curtis

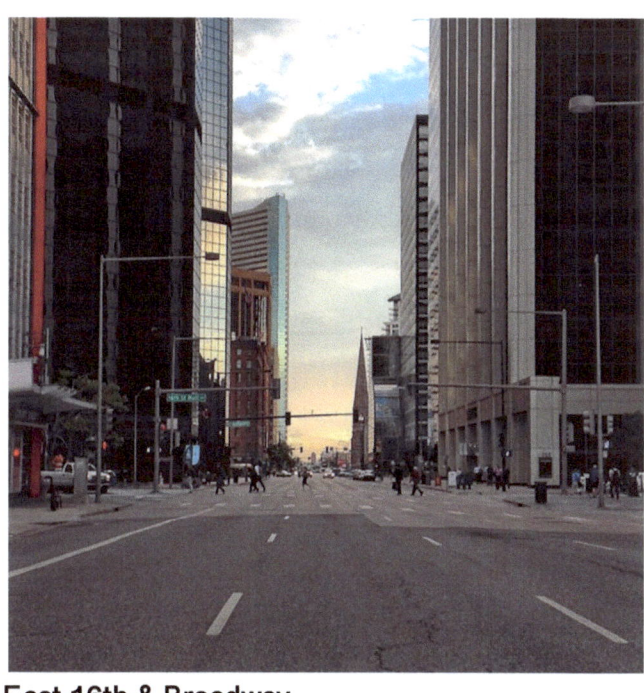

East 16th & Broadway

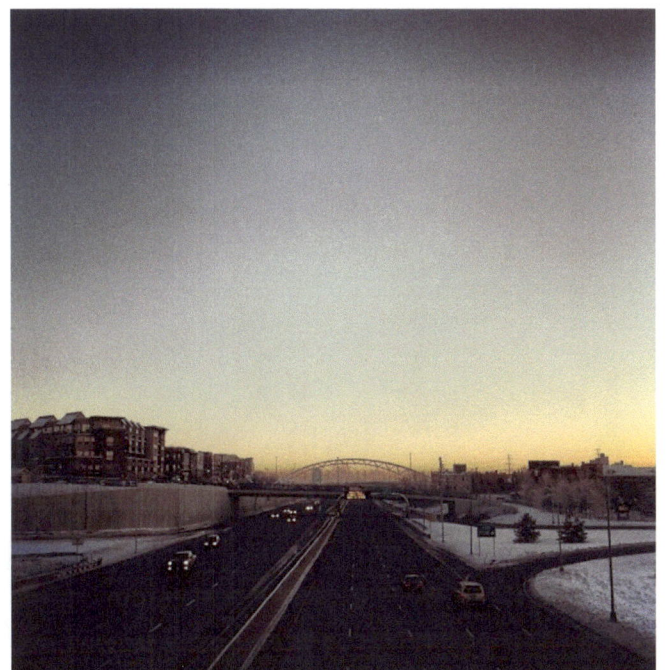

Speer Boulevard over I-25

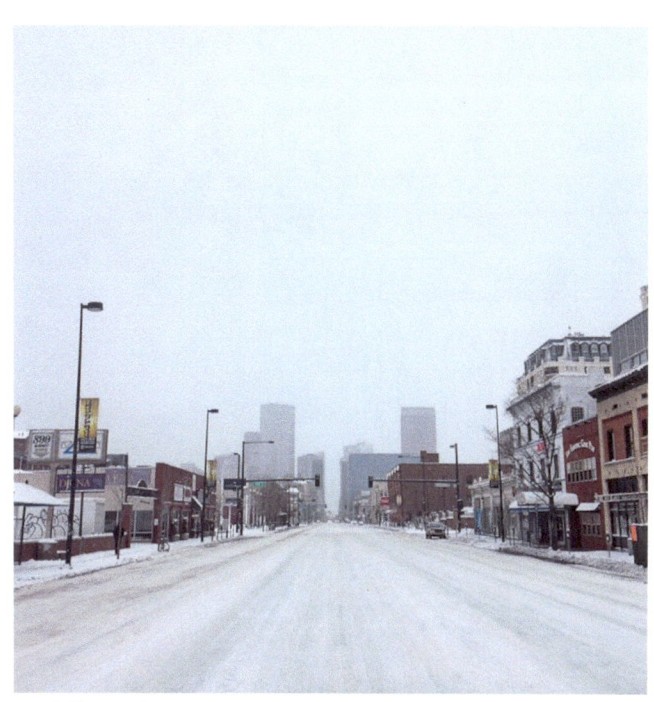

800 Broadway

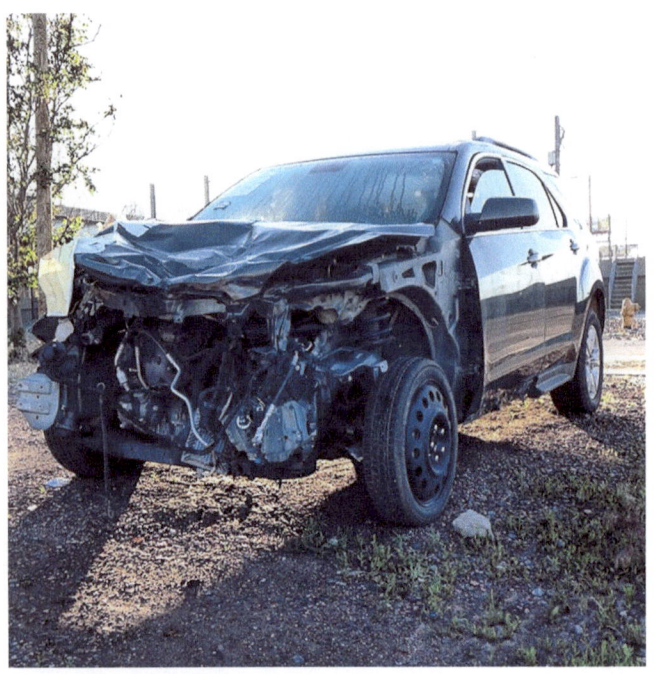

1801 West Colfax

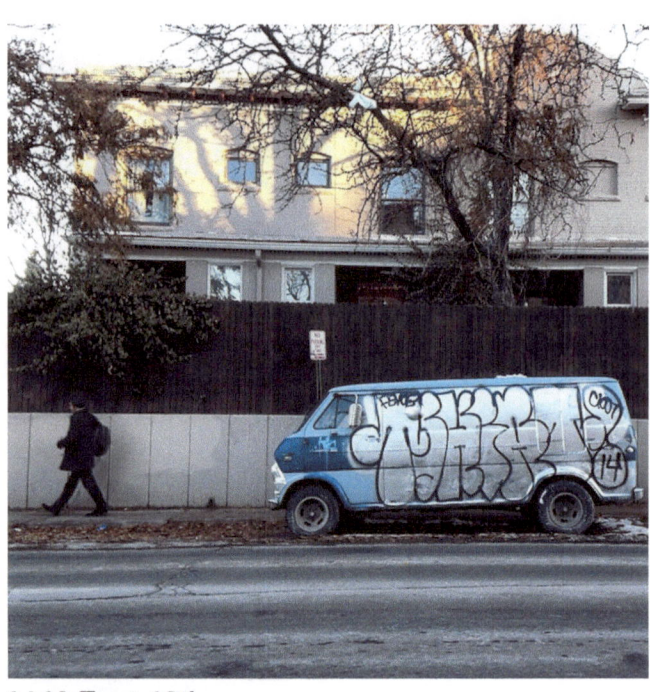

1116 East 13th

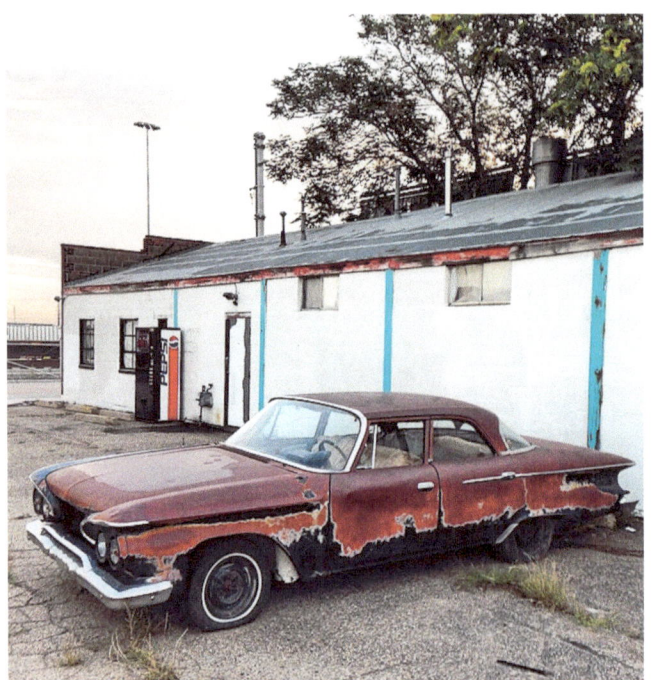

2190 East 40th

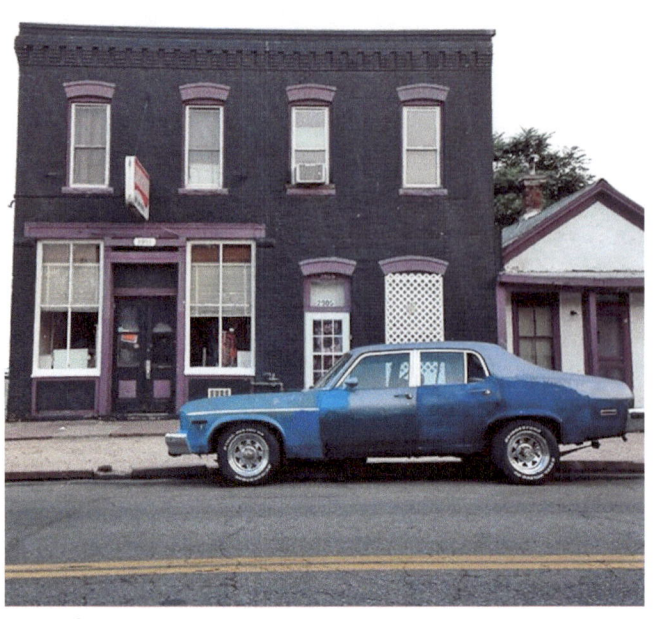

2901 Lawrence

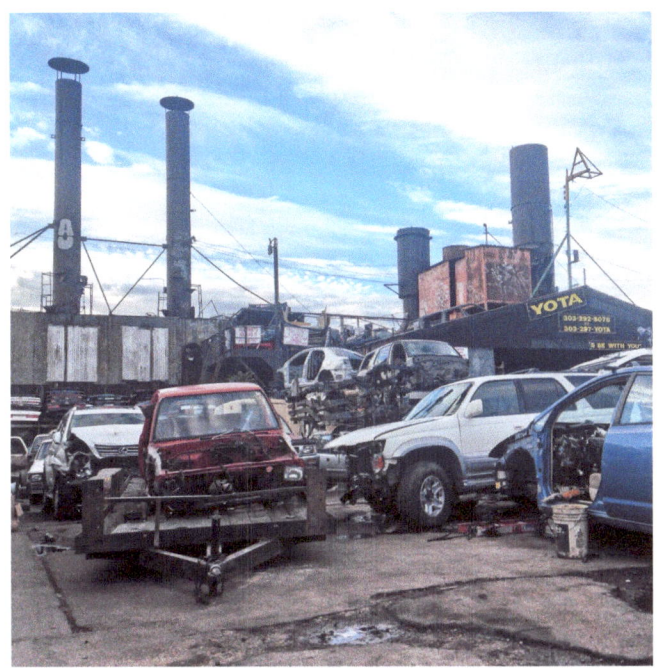

3134 Walnut

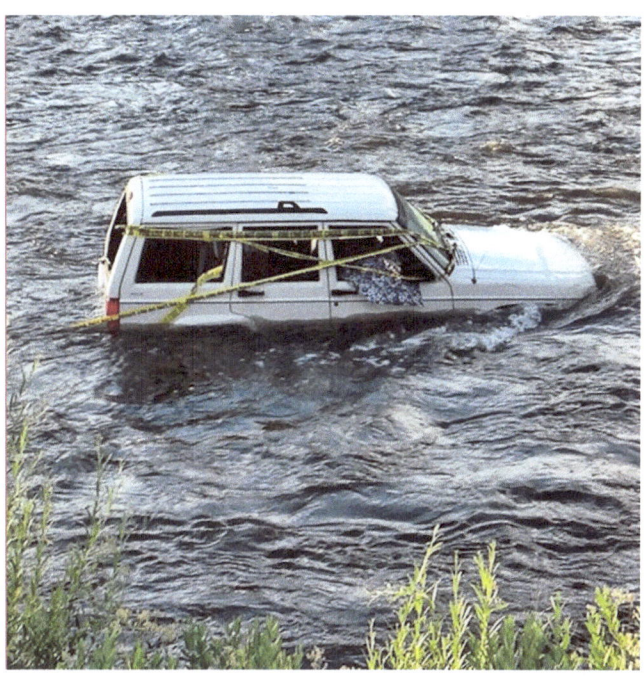

South Platte River between W Florida & W Evans

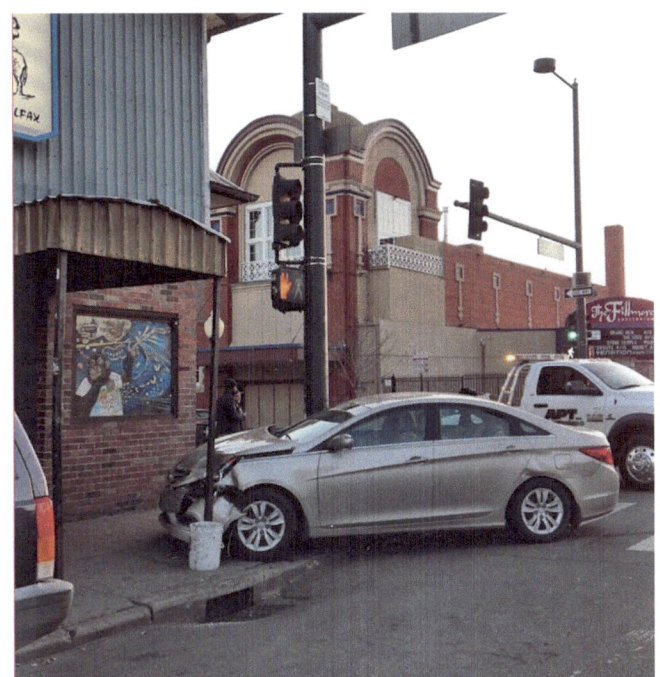

741 East Colfax

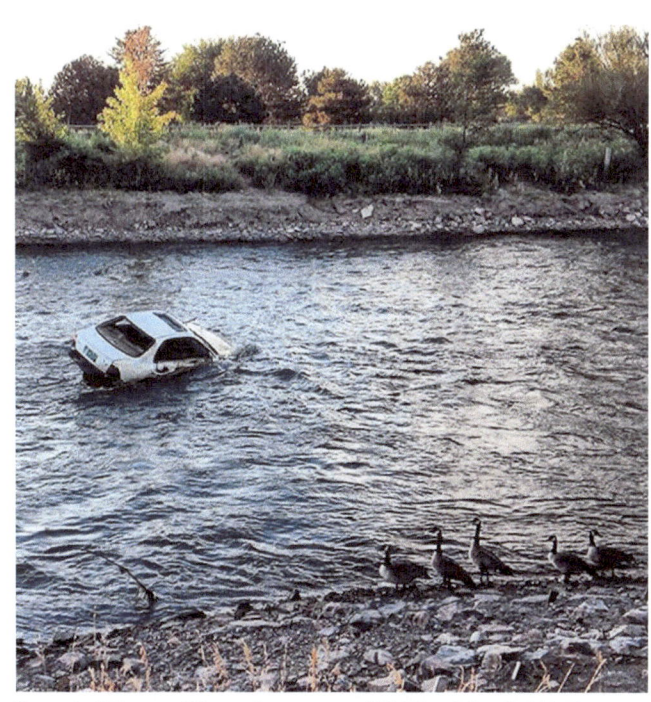

South Platte River between W Florida & W Evans

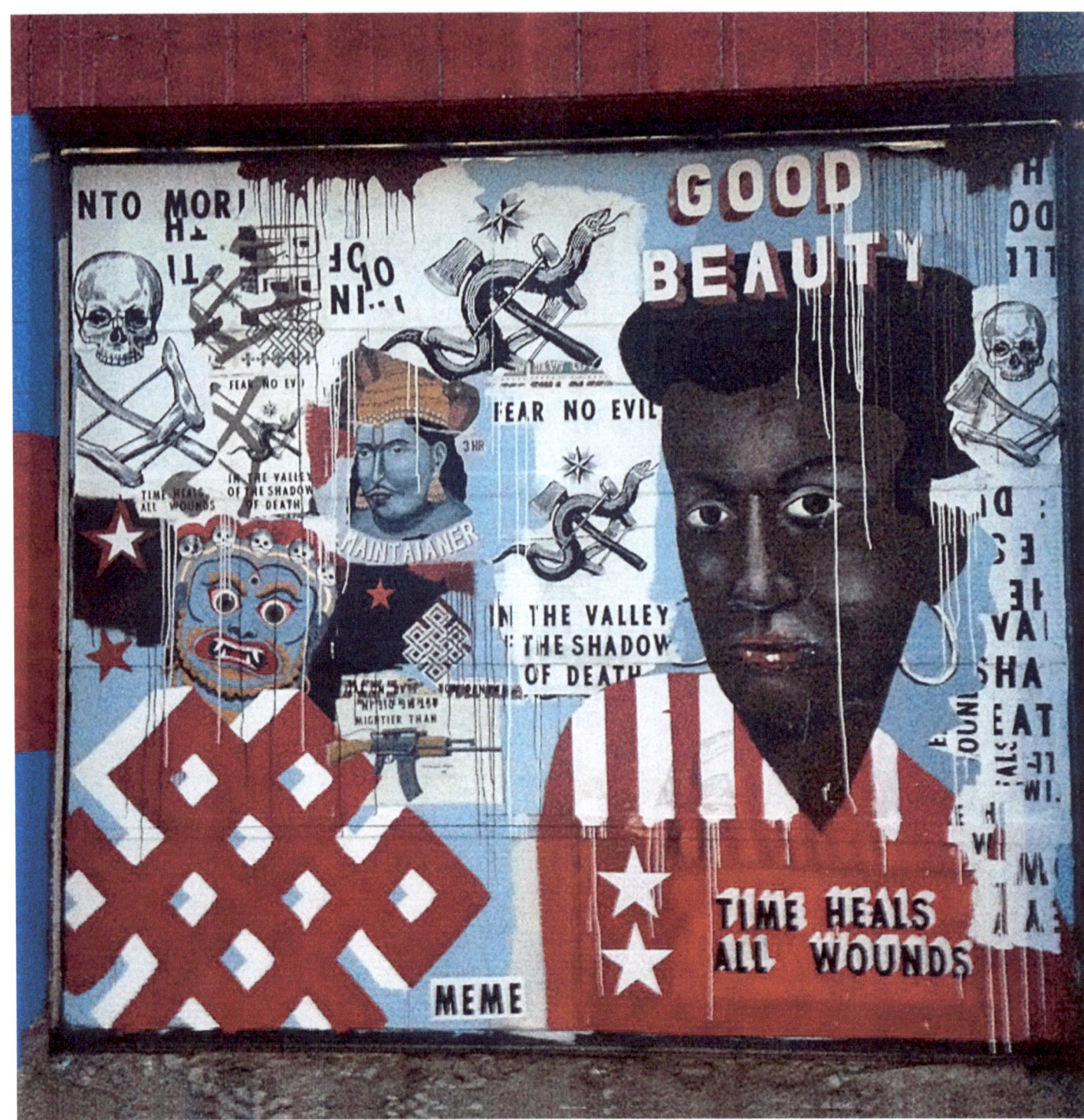

1801 East Colfax

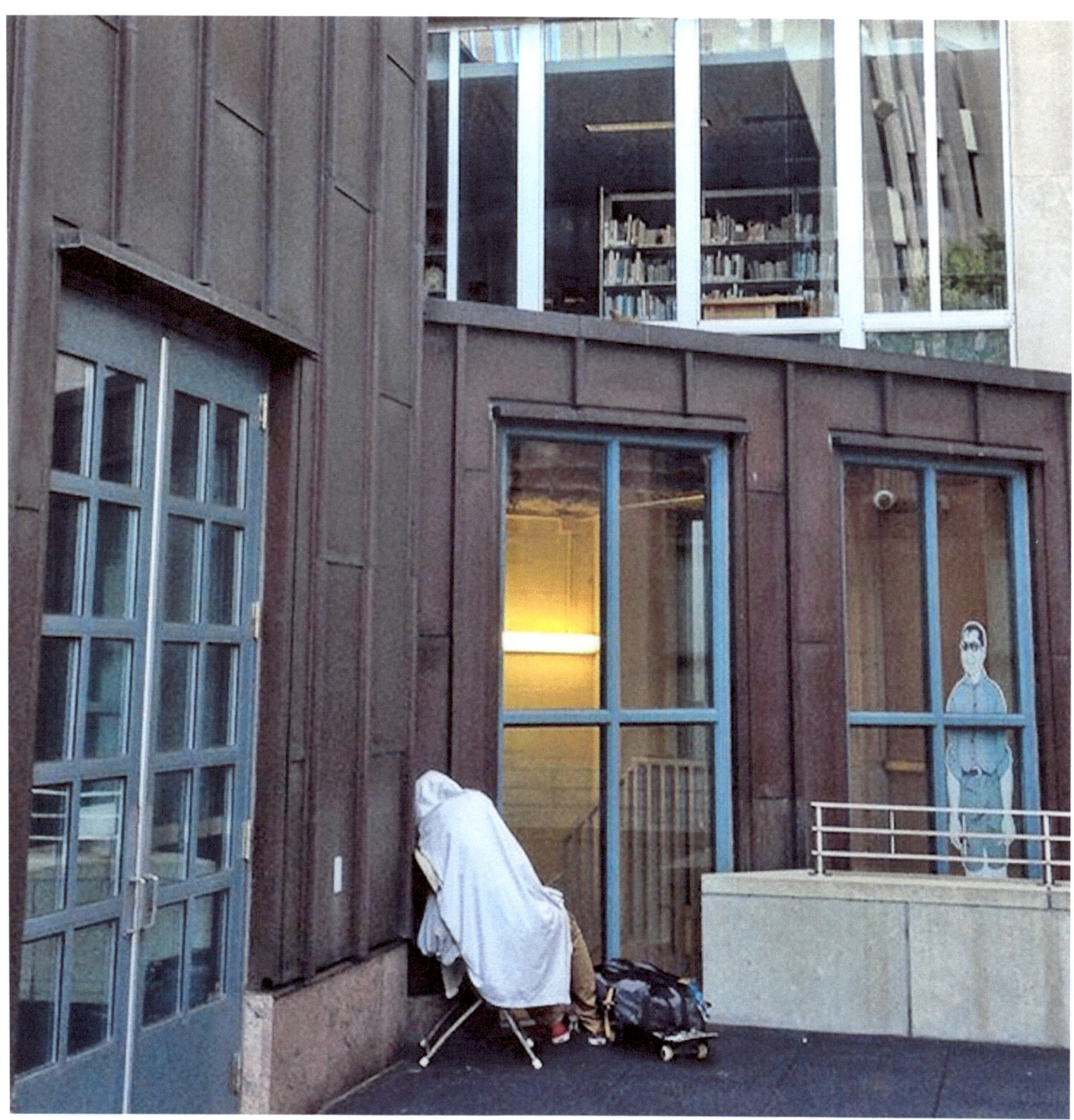

10 West 14th Avenue Parkway

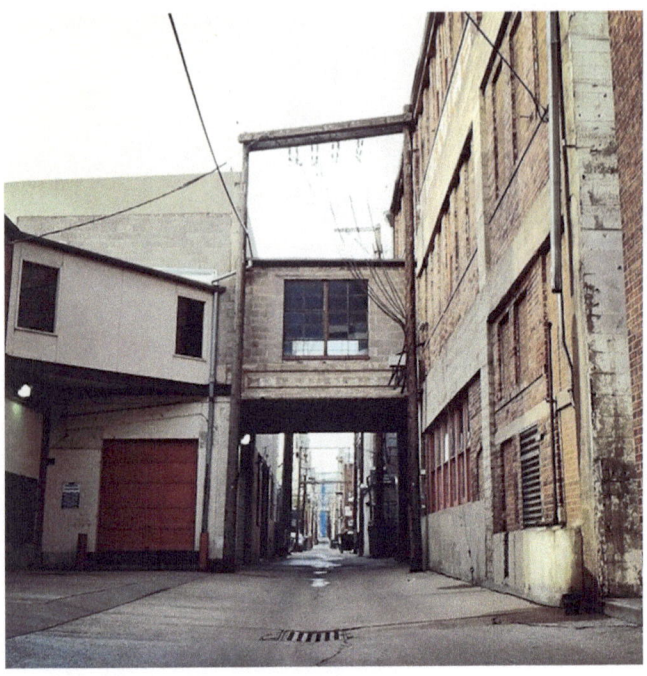

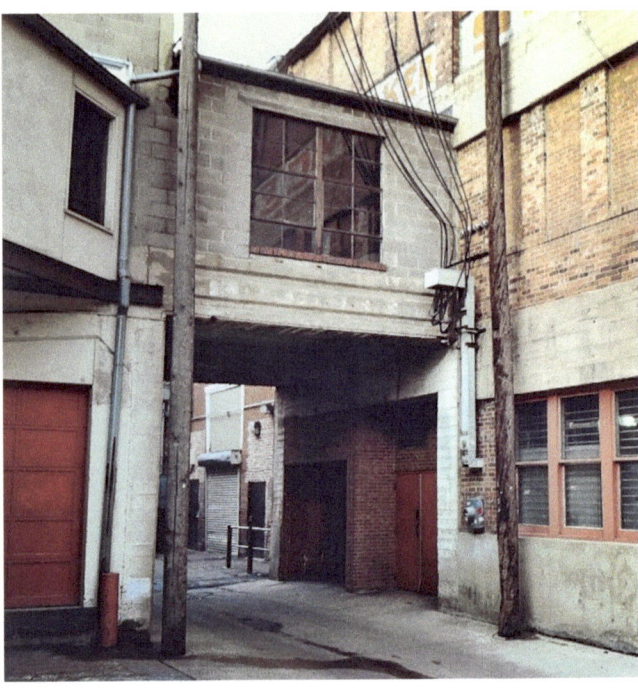

A few summers ago, I was driving from Montana back to Denver and for some reason, my mind kept focusing on comparing and contrasting Denver with New York City. New York is 230 years older than Denver, but the two cities have many parallels. Denver is a mere youngster in comparison to Manhattan and to large western cities like San Francisco. Certainly, that's one reason why Denver still struggles with growth and construction.

When you're diving south through Montana and Wyoming for hours on end, there is this moment where you see the Denver skyline way off in the distance. You get a similar feeling when you see Manhattan for the first time after driving through Connecticut, Vermont and Maine. It is inspiring and powerful, seeing a huge city approaching on the horizon.

Denver shares many architectural features in common with 19th century New York City, including its grid system, numbered streets, one-way thoroughfares and its many alleys. Another interesting feature they have in common is the Bandit's Roost. In the squalor of the Lower East Side, before the turn of the century, long before zoning and city inspectors existed, people built their own additions onto and above public streets. The Bandit's Root was a unique architectural feature of Manhattan; it was a room or single corridor connecting two buildings above a public alley.

Groups of thieves could exploit the feature by working together. They might direct a lost box truck driver or a hapless stagecoach into their dark alley. As soon as the vehicle was parked and its driver distracted, the thieves waiting above in the Bandit's Roost would quickly and silently open the windows (or secret panels), reach down and lift up the cargo, and then escape through the connecting side buildings. By the time the driver realized he'd been robbed, it was too late. His vehicle stripped of its contents, the thieves long gone, and the driver clueless as to how the whole thing happened.

Denver has a few examples of the Bandit's Roost, and a couple are true Bandit's Roosts because private companies own them. Denver has more Bandit's Roosts than Portland and Minneapolis, and the last time Manhattan had one, Teddy Roosevelt was President.

Speaking of the 19th century New York, my approach to photography for this project was highly influenced by a New Yorker from that era: Jacob Riis. In the 1890s, when Riis and his small team of assistants were shooting photos for his famous exposé, How the Other Half Lives, they came up with an interesting photography tactic. Sometimes they paid their subjects to sit still, but they preferred to obtain the "raw" photos of the subject in action — sitting in the squalor of their lodging house, lurking in the dark shadows. Riis knew how much more effective his message became when it reflected reality as opposed to when they posed people and created it artificially.

Riis would get people to agree to be photographed, but then he wouldn't announce when he was going to start. He would fidget with his camera while talking, behaving as if here were merely adjusting his settings. Then suddenly he would take a photo like a thief — as fast as possible. The momentary flashbulb and smoke would confuse the subject and while in a

a haze of their confusion, Riis and his colleagues would escape into the night without saying a word.

For me, this tactic was a working model that I used each night. I didn't want to talk about my photography. The people who caught me taking pictures seemed indifferent, but one guy did yell at me: "Why the hell you takin' pictures of the street?!" I wasn't even sure how to answer him. It seemed too complex and long-winded to explain myself or describe what I was doing calmly or to yell anything in response.

Who has the time to explain the things we get into or make sense of this behavior. I dont. I got paid to take pictures all over Denver and I like exploring. That's what I'm doing taking pictures of the street, sir.

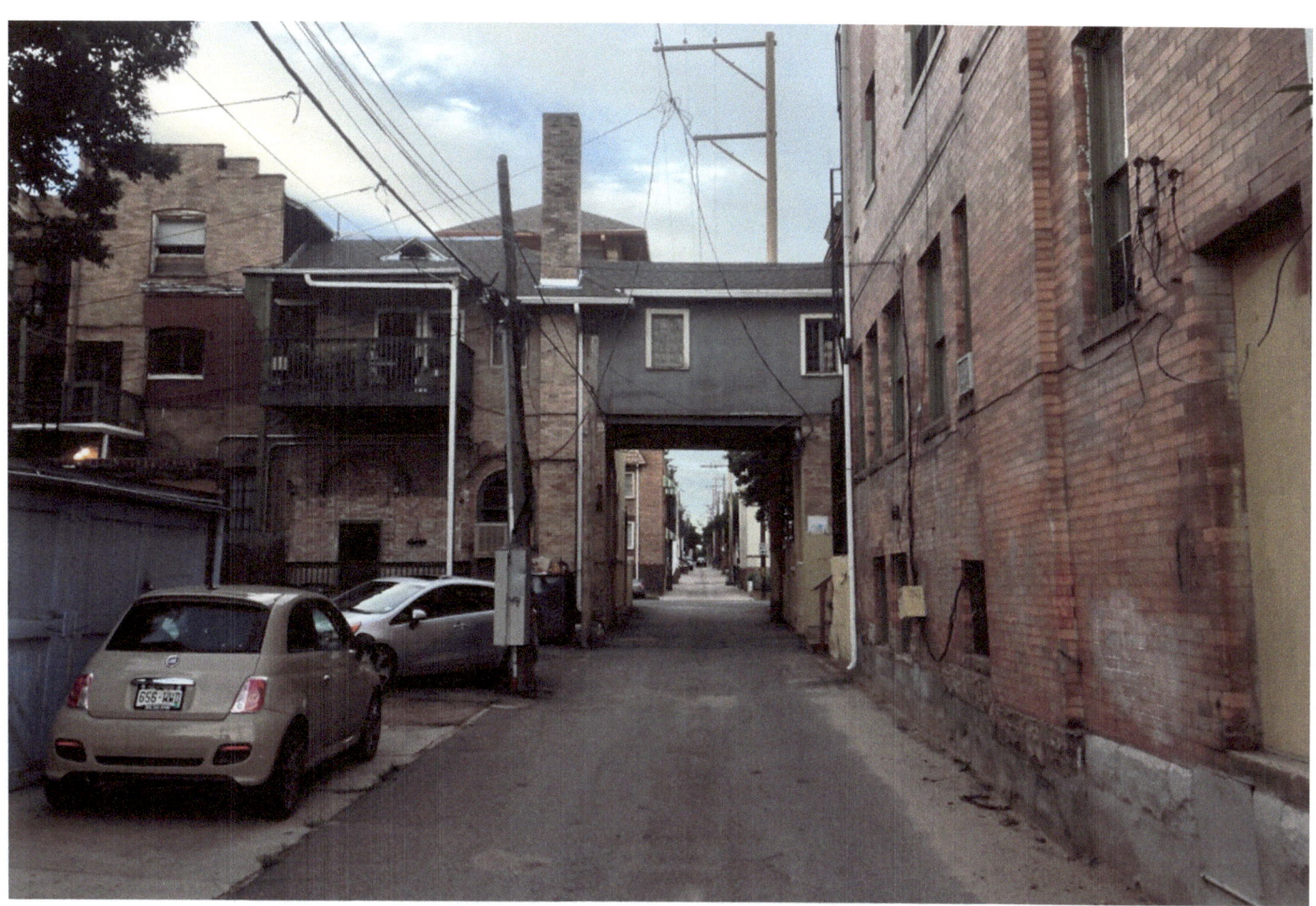

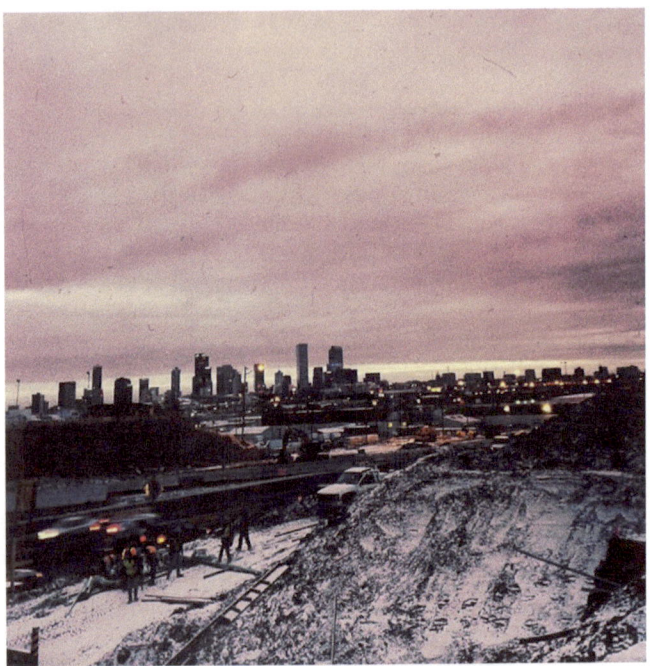

6th Avenue / I-25 on-ramp at Federal

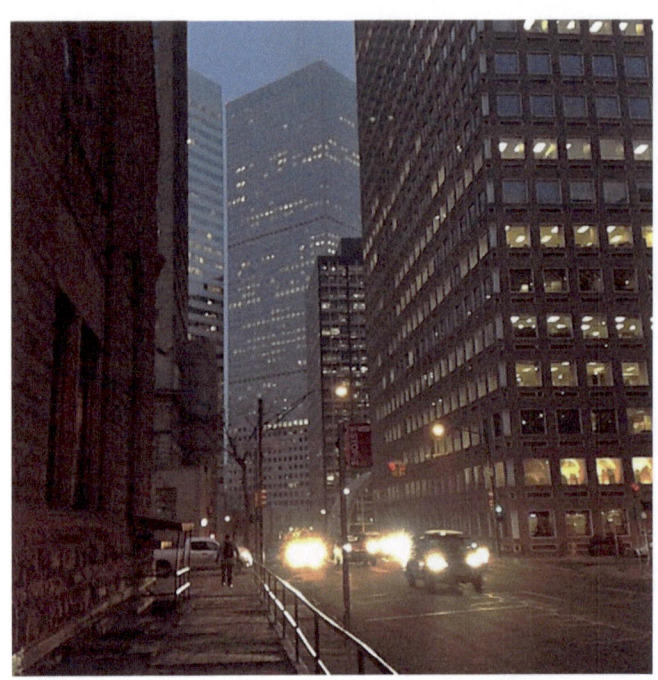

17th & Sherman

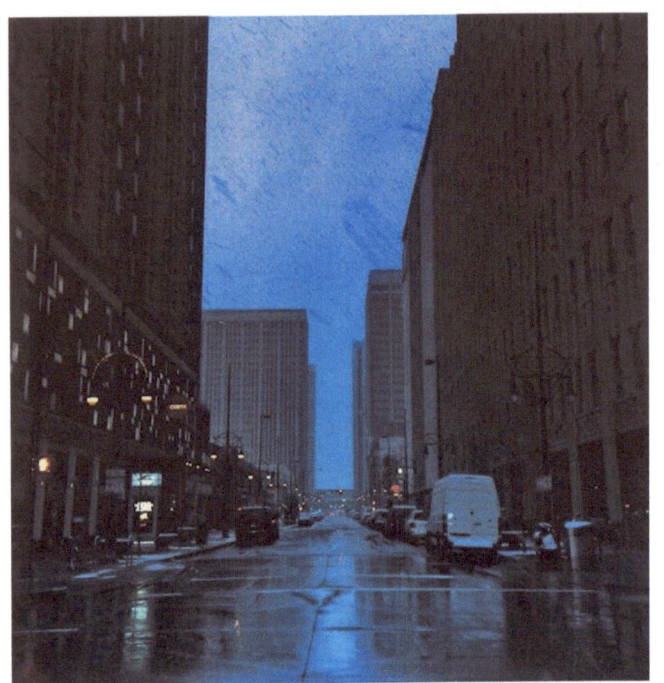

14th & Curtis

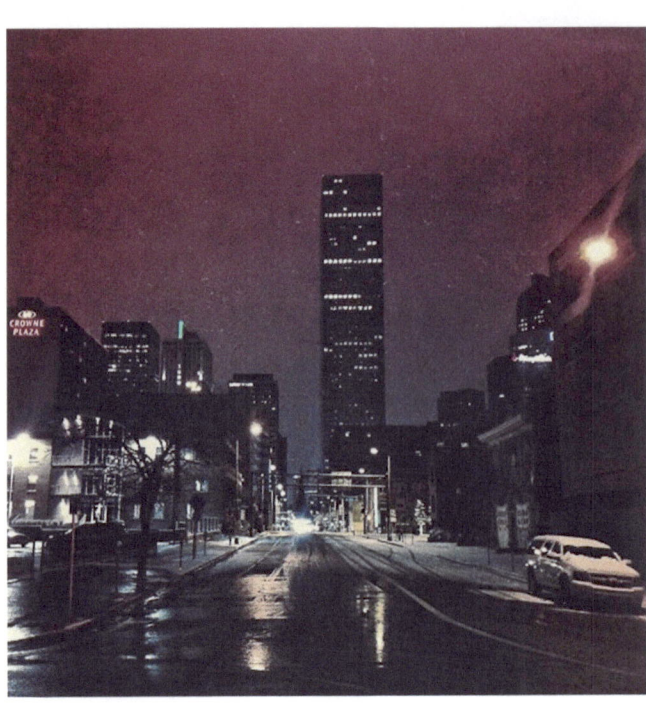

13th & Tremont

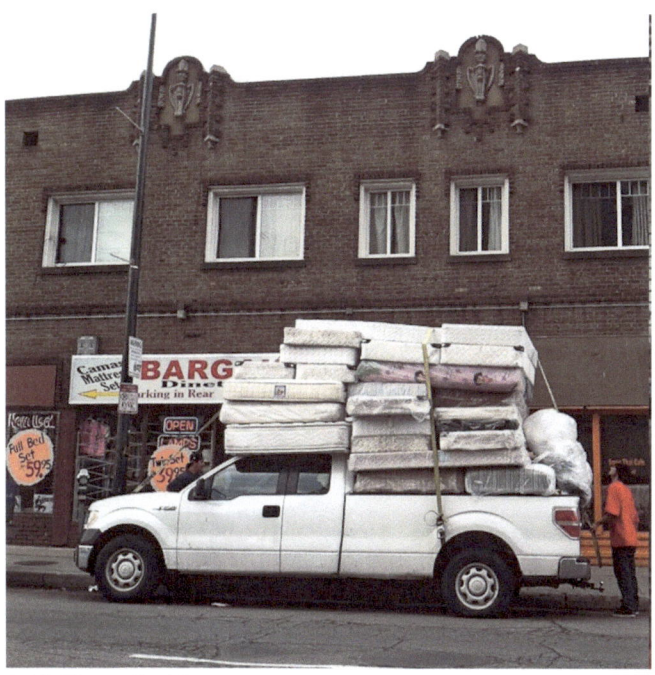

410 East Colfax

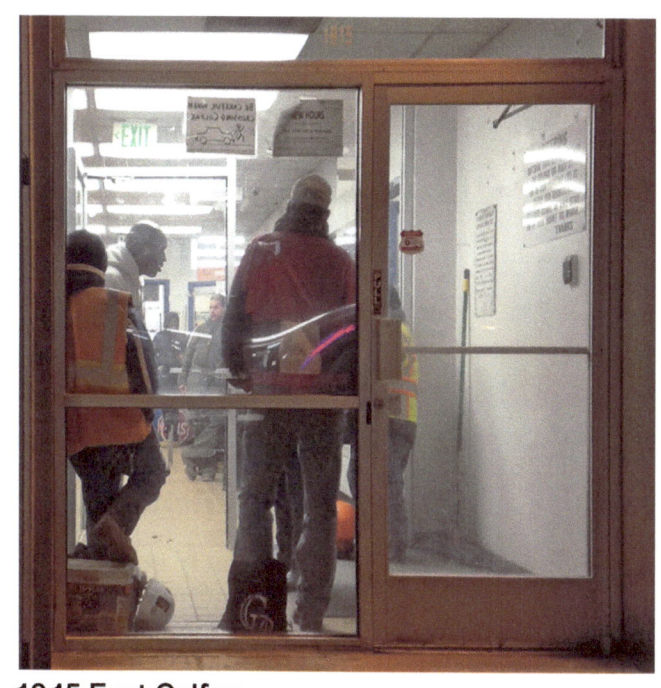

1915 East Colfax

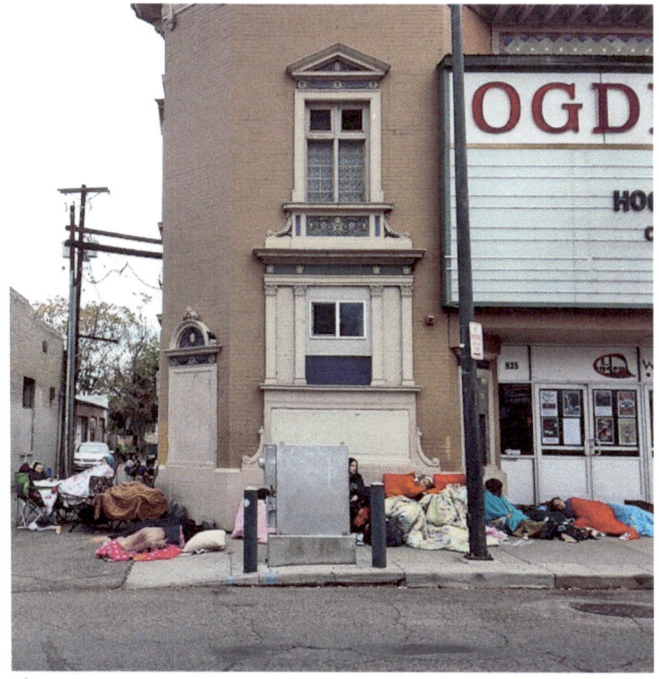

935 East Colfax

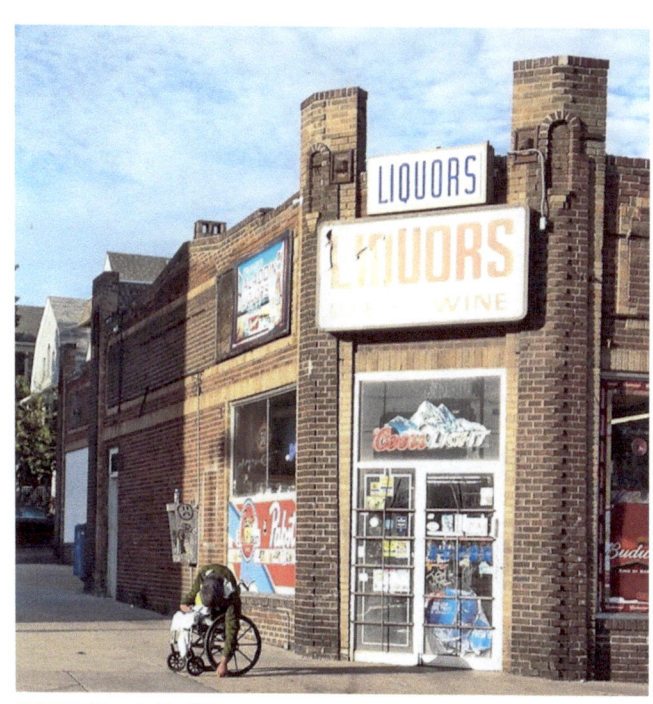

2032 East Colfax

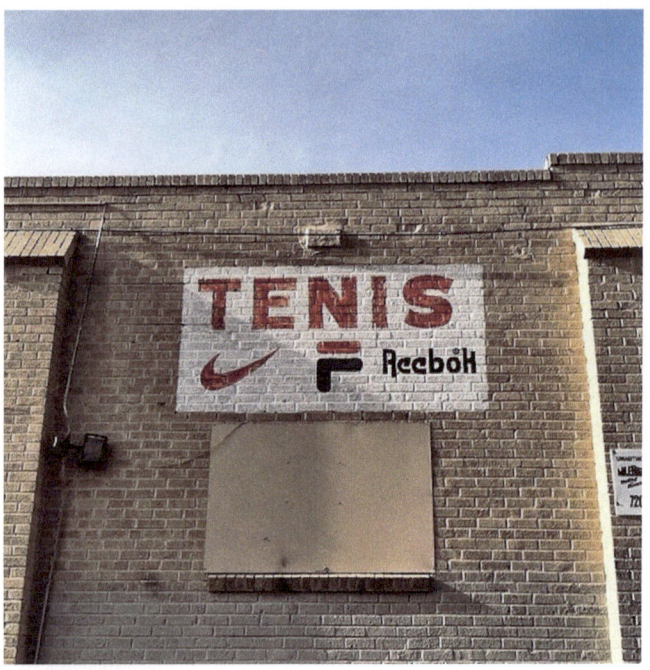

816 Federal

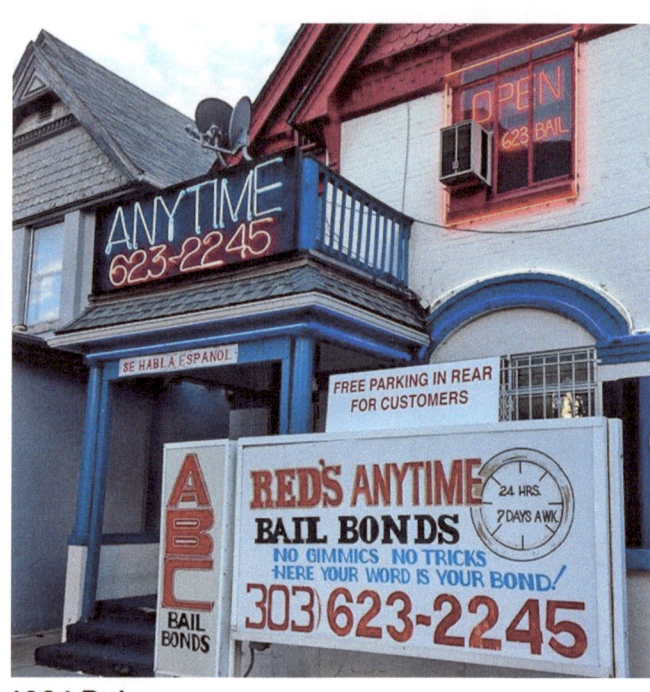

1321 Delaware

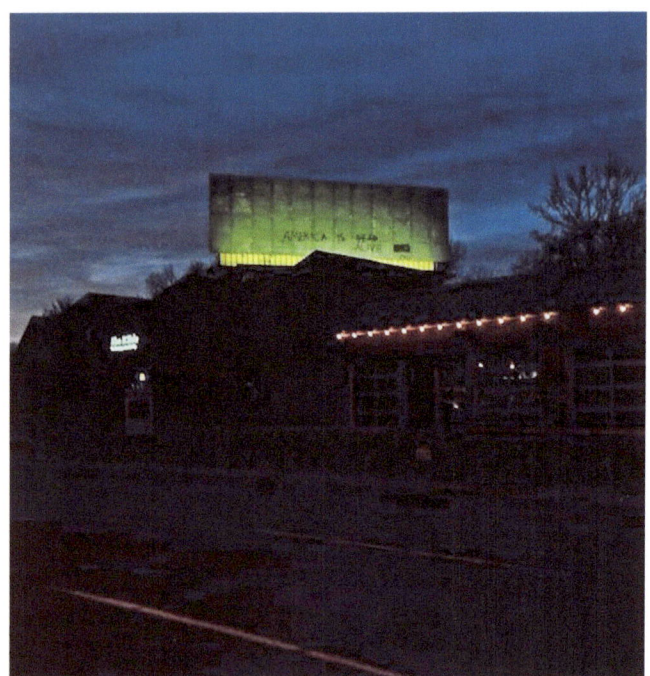

East 17th & North Lafayette

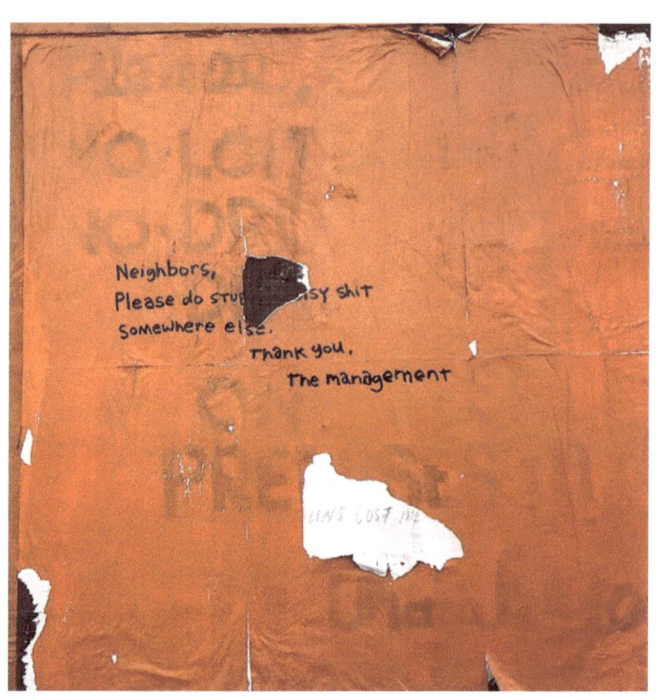

Somewhere in LoDo

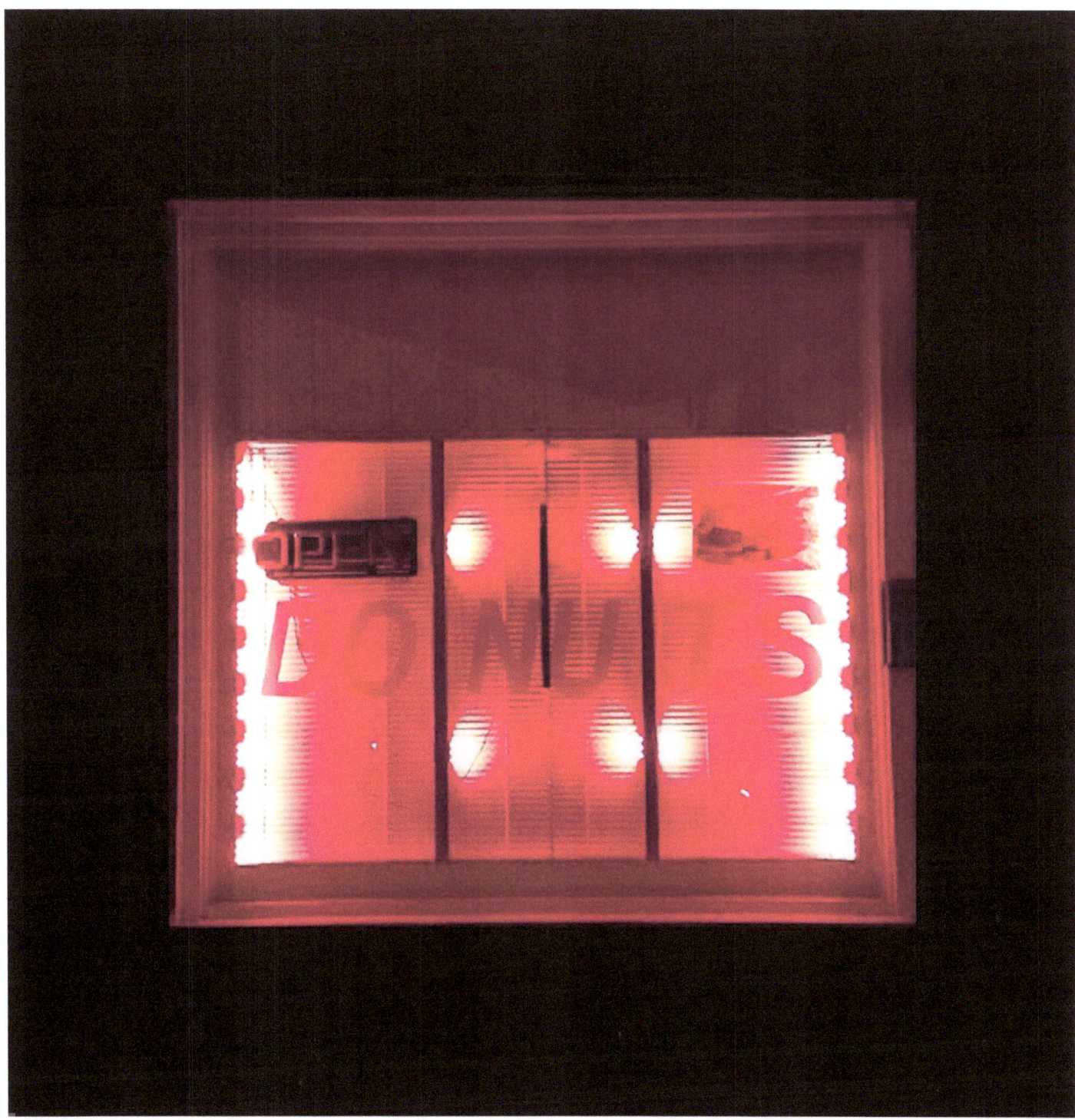

2855 York

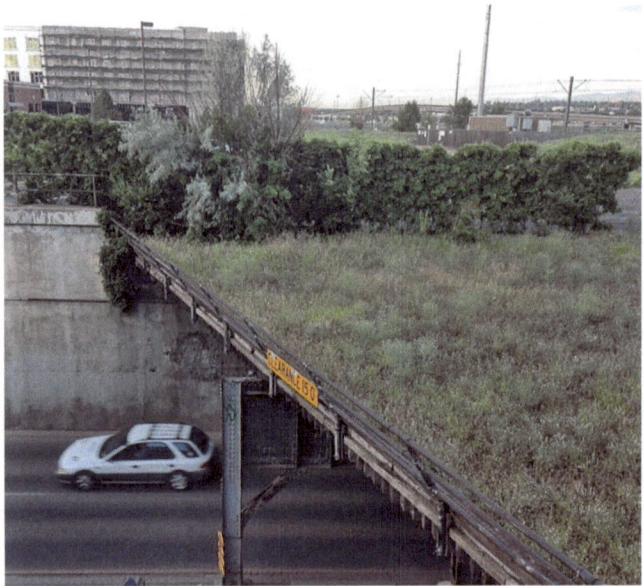
W Mississippi between S Bannock & S Acoma

Those green and white Colorado "NATIVE" stickers have stirred up a lot of controversy, locally, in the comment section of news articles and around dinner tables. Their very existence says something about Coloradoans.

When I was a kid growing up in Catholic school in New Jersey, I was taught by old school Italians and nuns with large wooden rulers that you can only have pride in something if you personally achieved it. Otherwise, your pride was really just vanity, and vanity was something to be avoided at all costs. Vanity was up there with sin and shame and snake charmers.

They taught us that people who were proud to be Italian or proud to be American were foolish and embarrassing because they didn't have a hand in deciding to be any of those things. On the other hand, people who were proud of their report cards or bowling scores were allowed to boast because those were things they had accomplished themselves. They warned us that pride, mixed with ego, usually leads to bad things. What do people have to gain from being exclusionary? I'm not really sure.

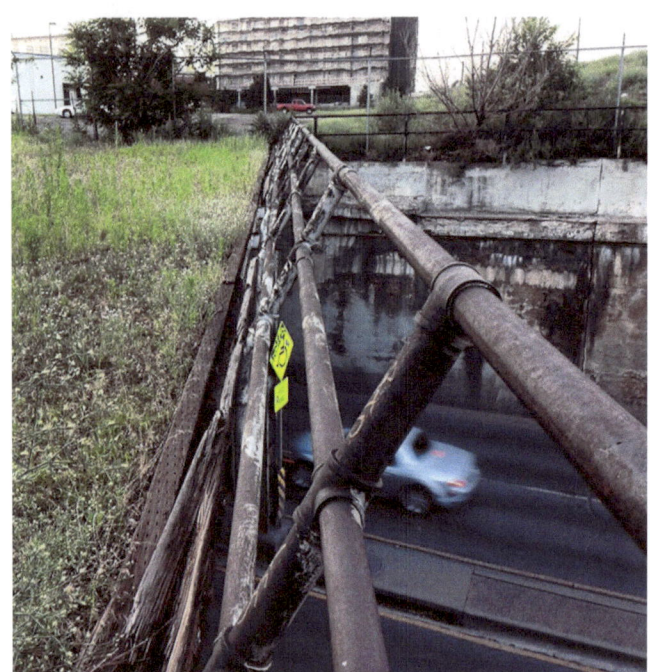
W Mississippi between S Bannock & S Acoma

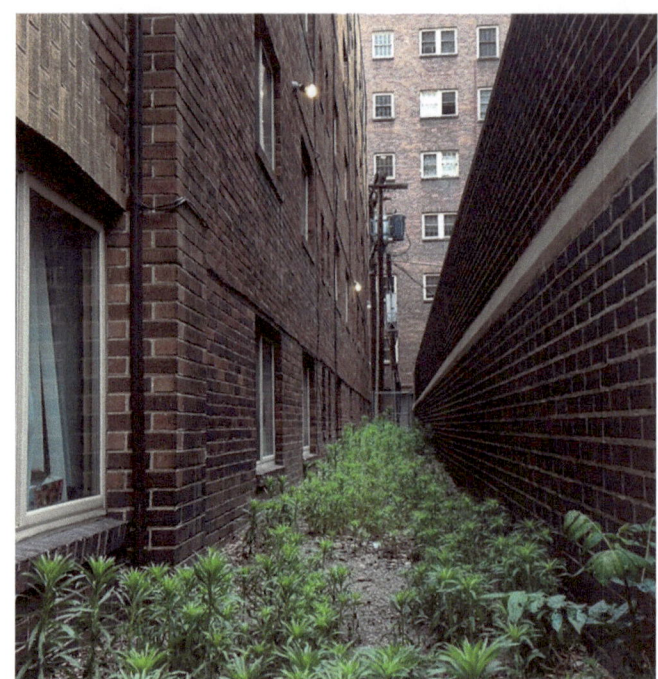
Grant St

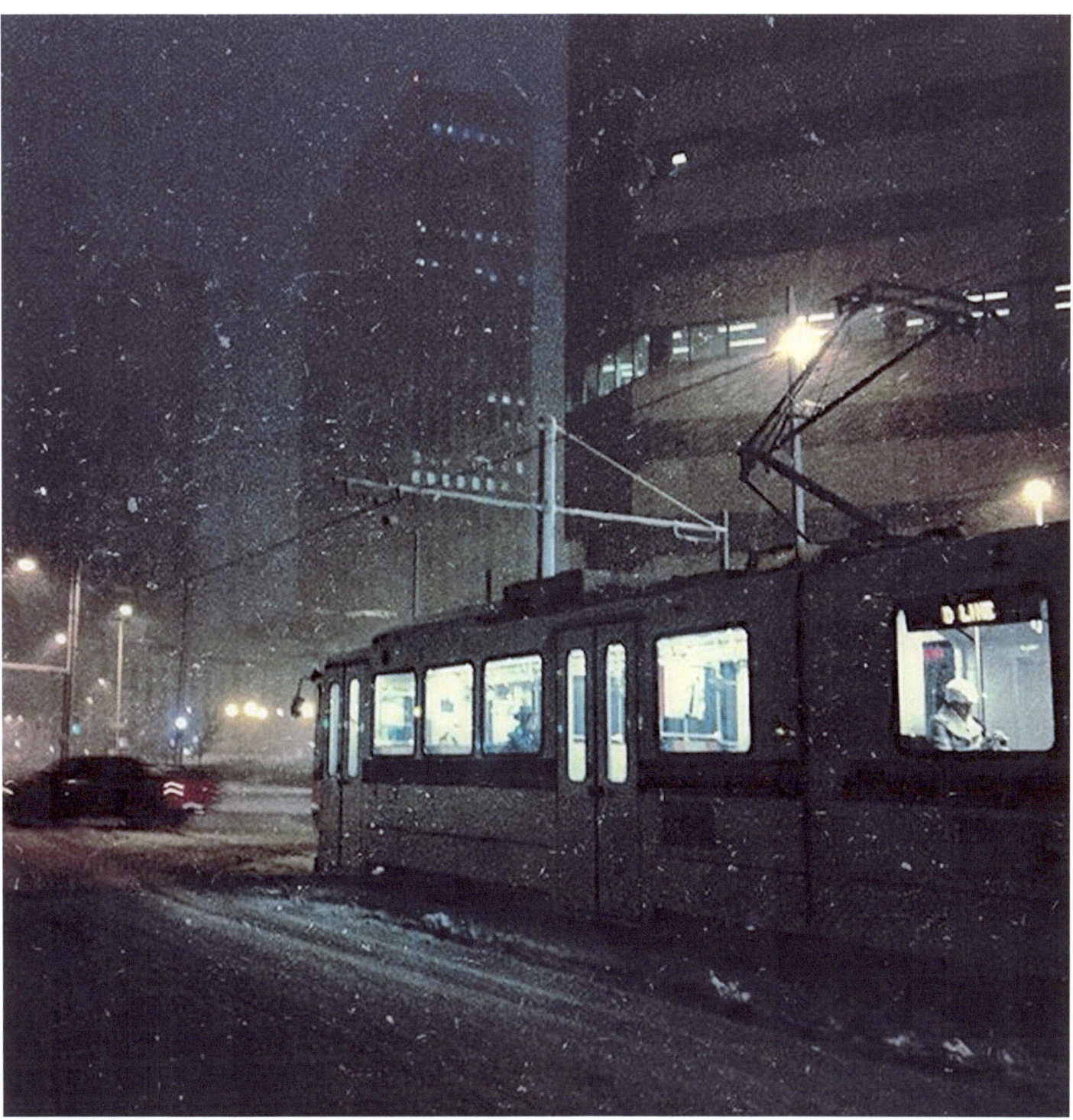

1627 California

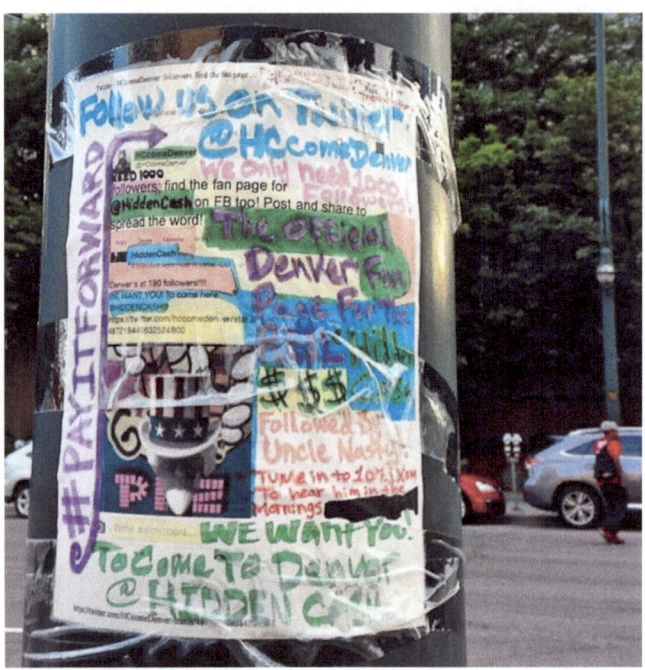

1200 17th

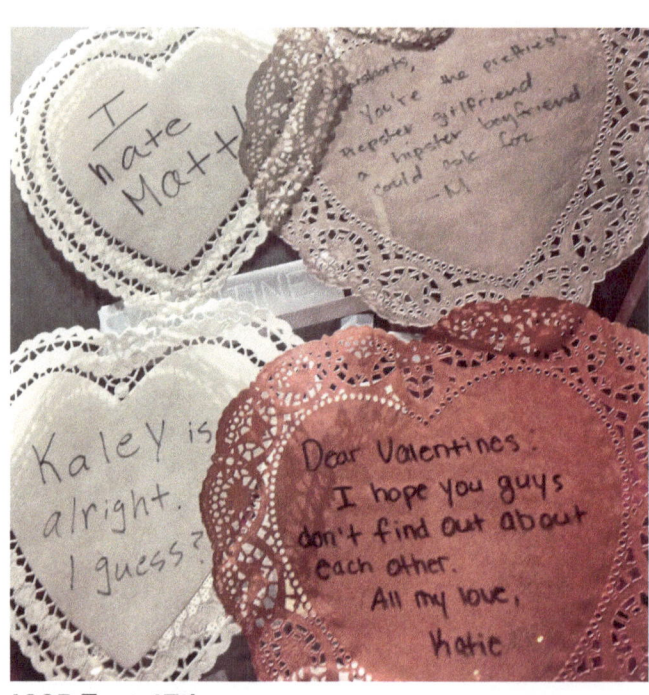

1225 East 17th

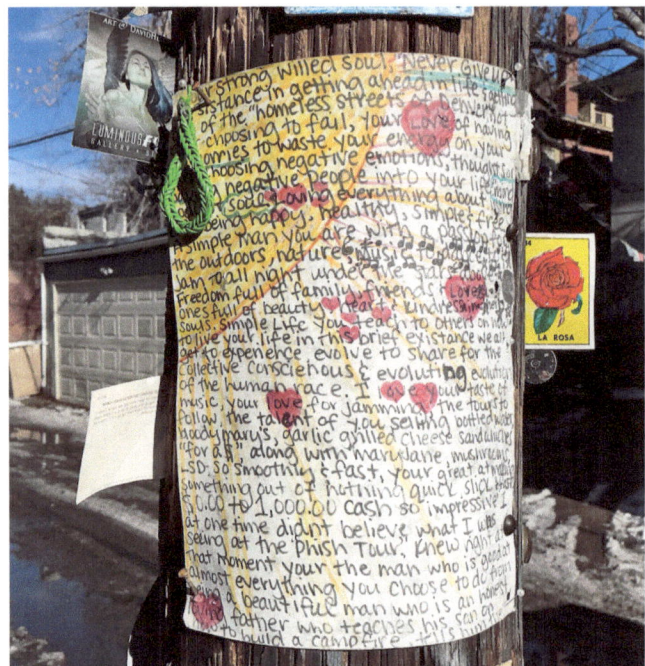

13th Avenue alley between Lafayette and Marion

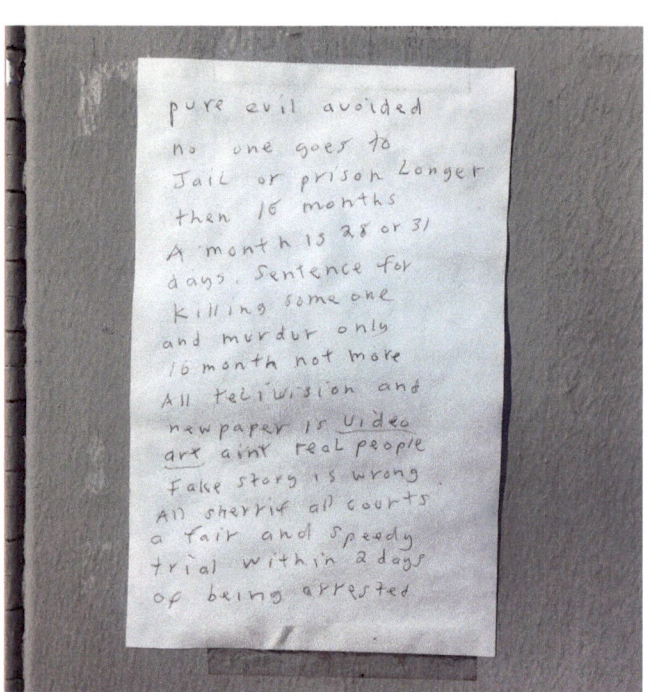

East 17th & Franklin

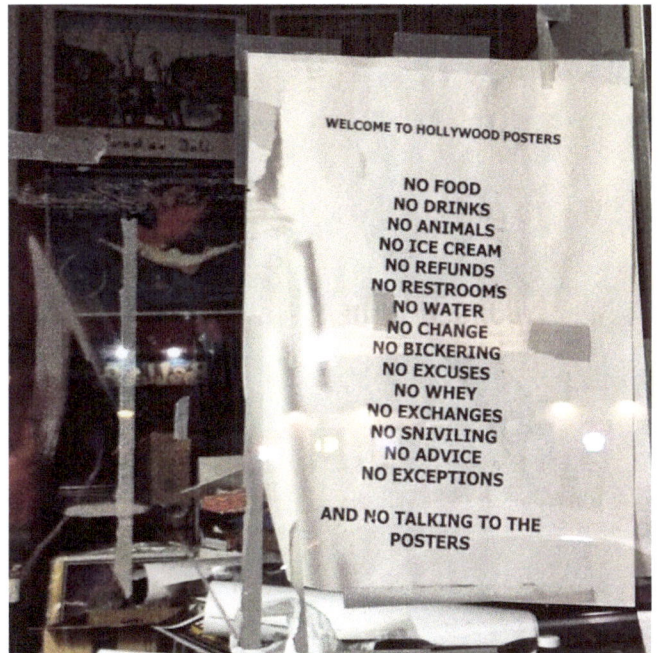

326 East Colfax

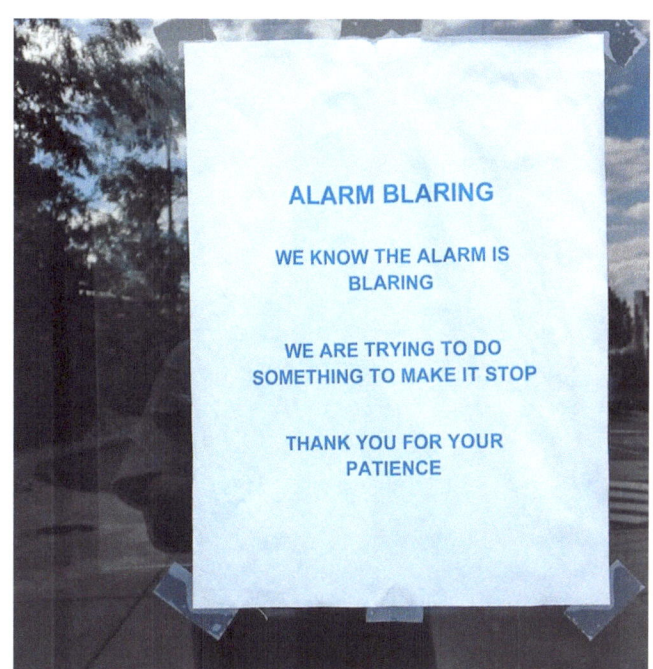

Somewhere Uptown

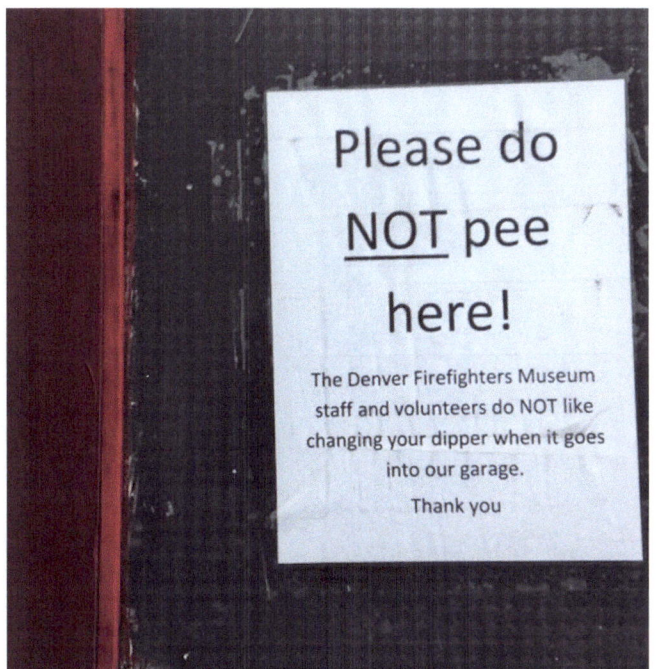

1326 Tremont

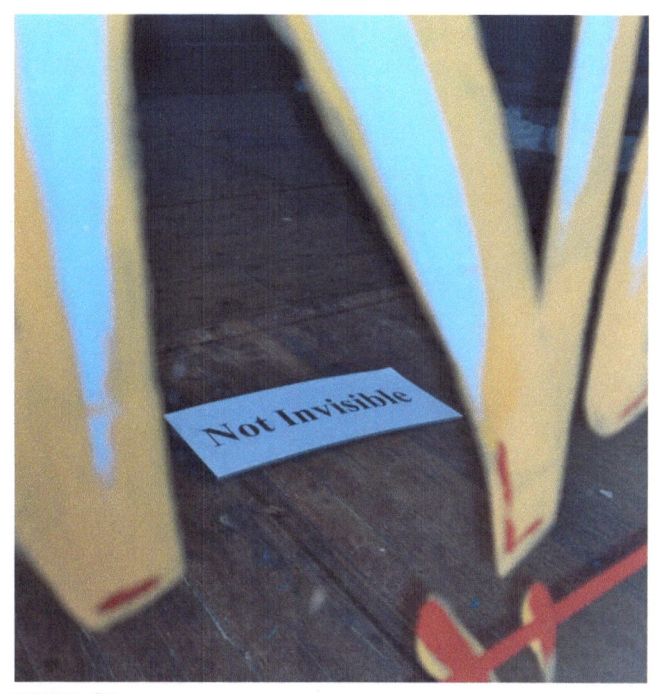

2255 Champa

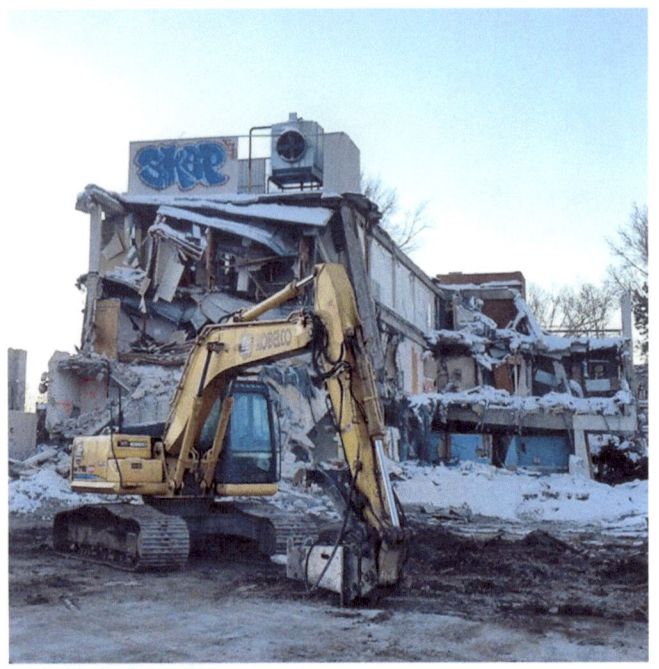

1655 North Lafayette

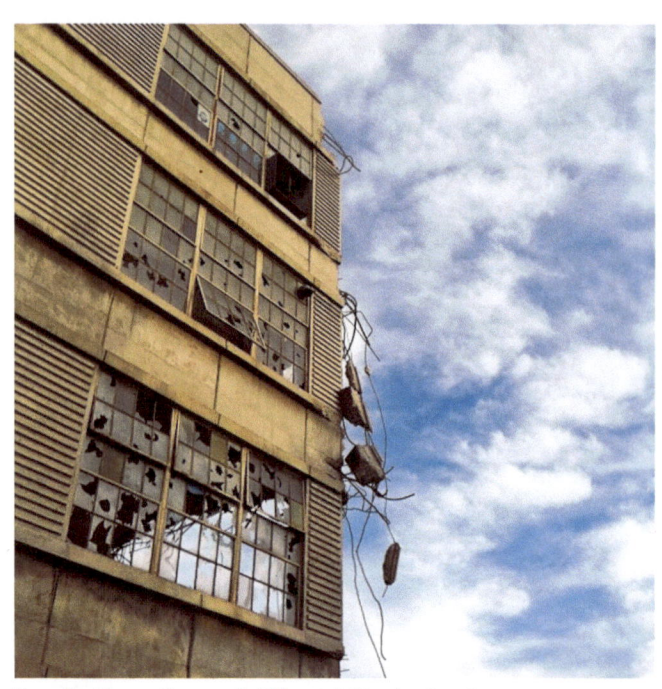

South Broadway & West Mississippi

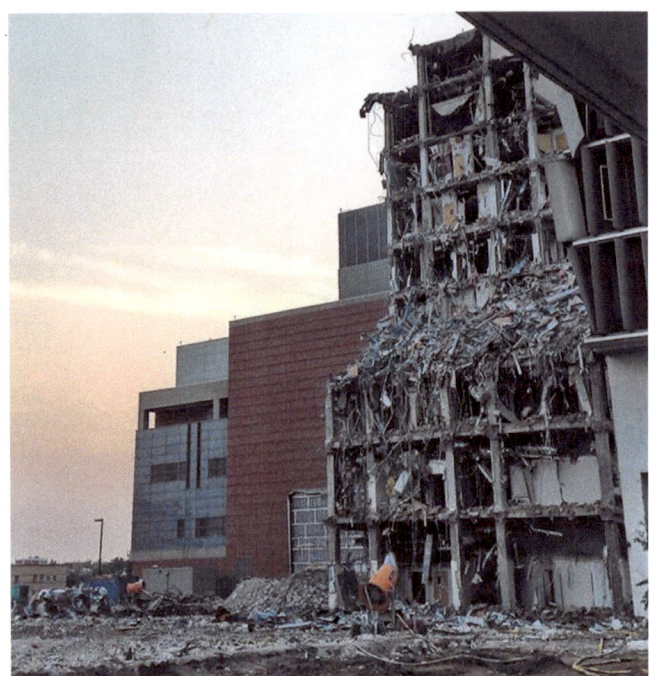

4198 E 9th

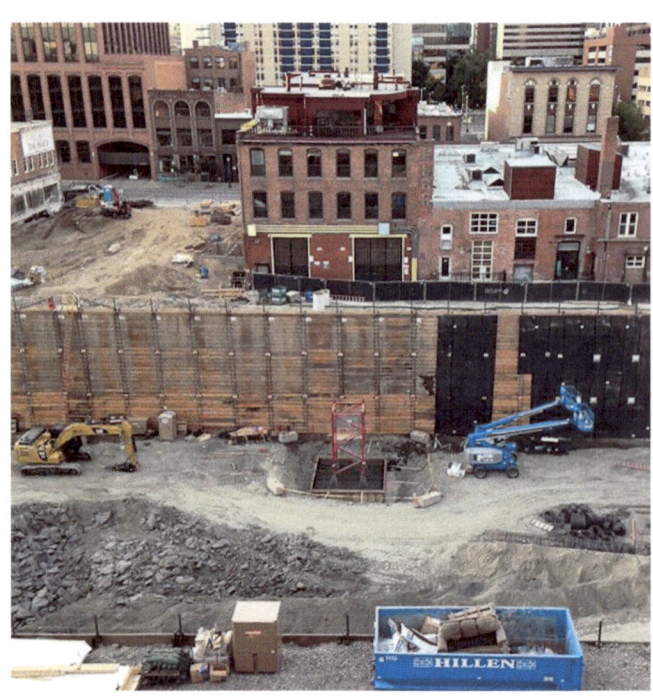

1800 Wazee

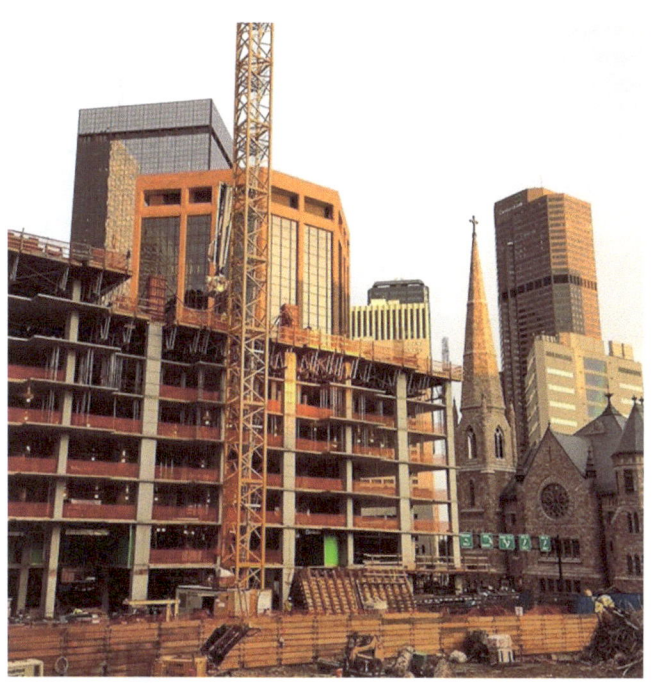

1776 Broadway

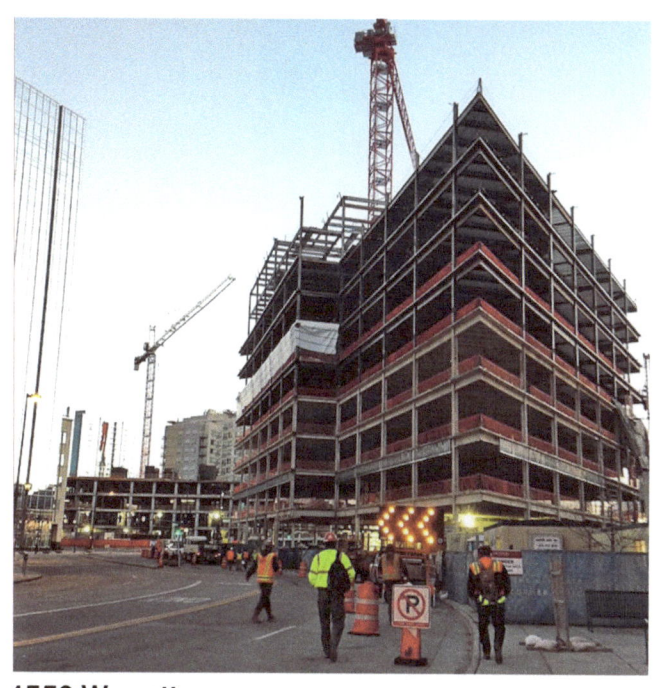

1550 Wewatta

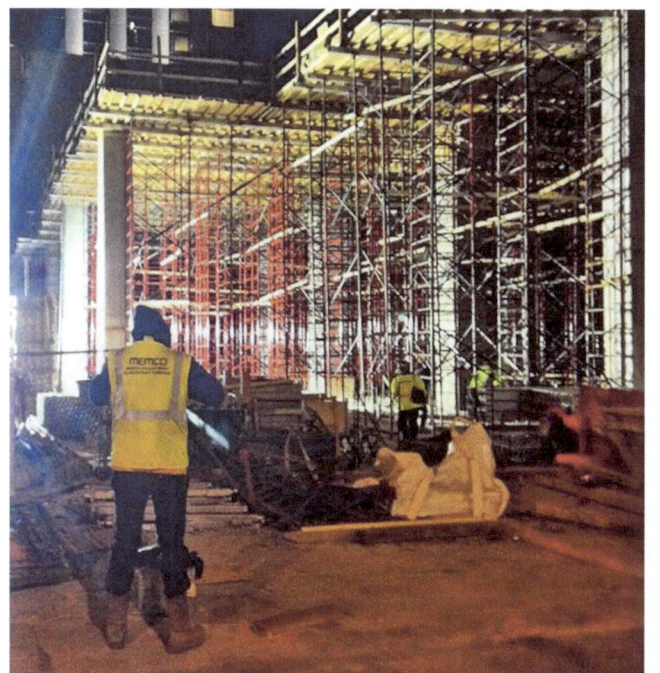

1144 15th

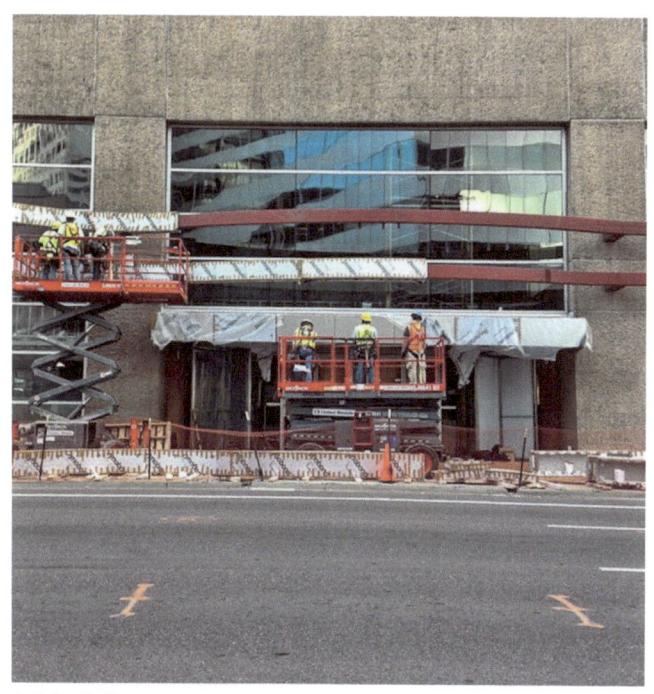

17th & Broadway

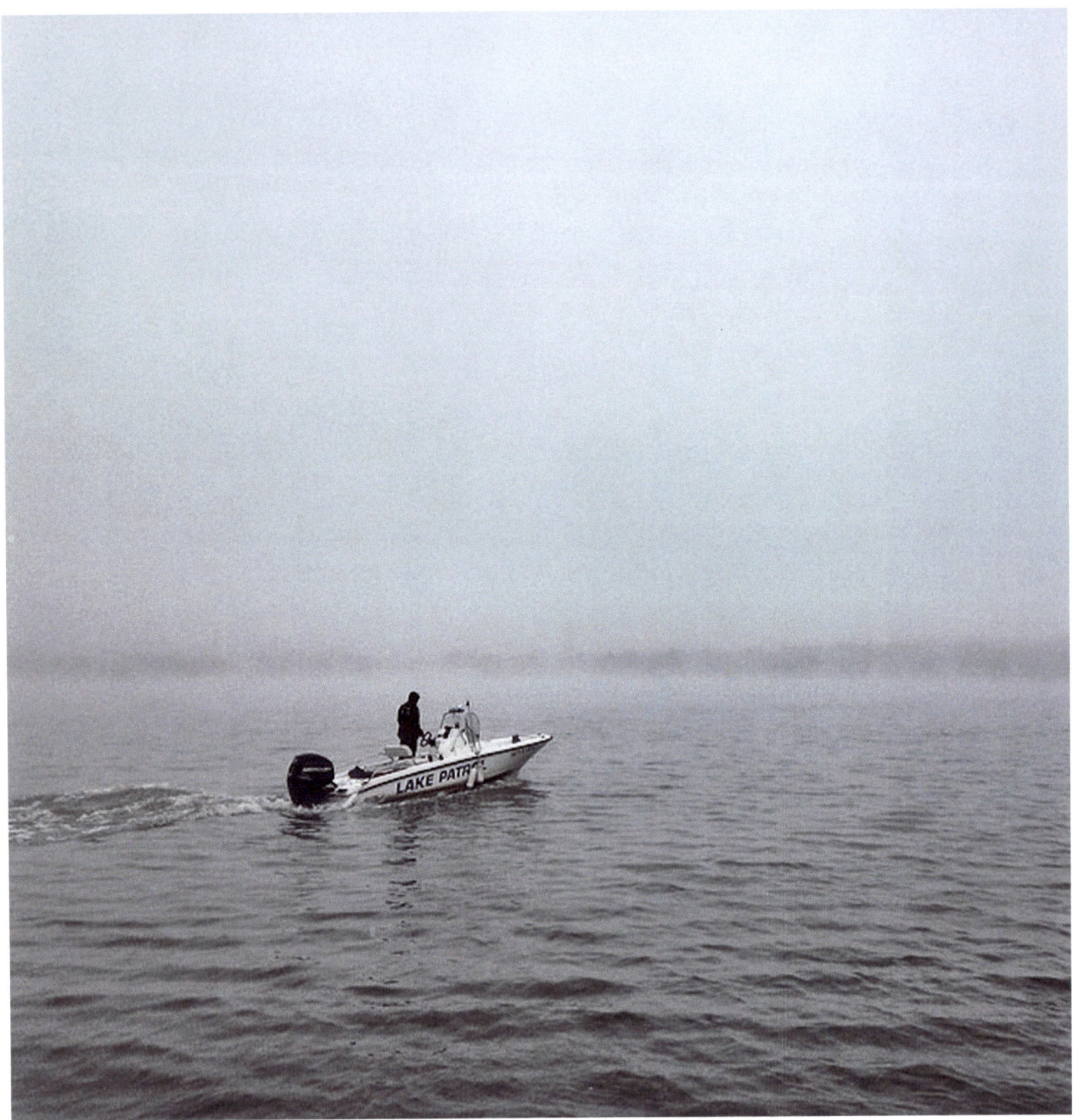

Sloan Lake

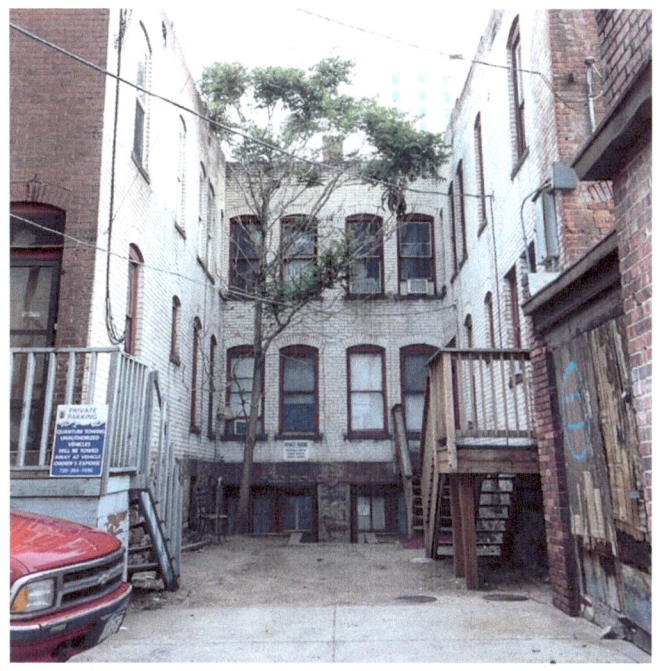

Classified

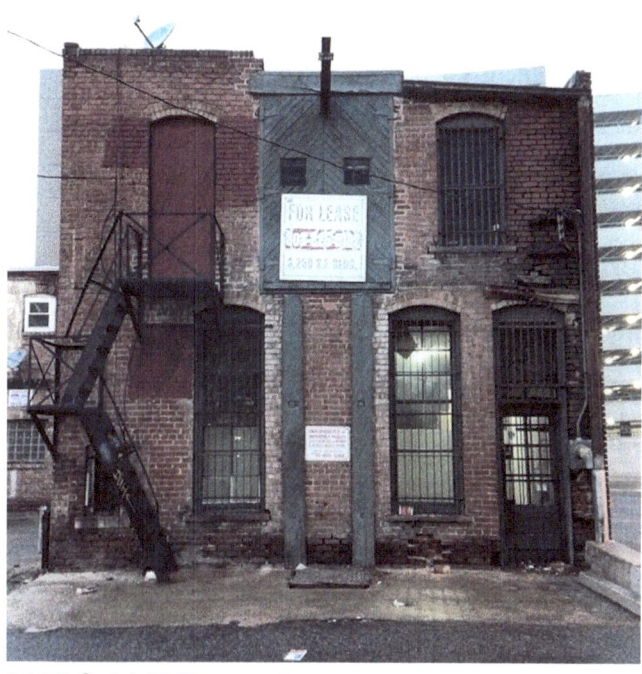

1438 & 1440 Tremont

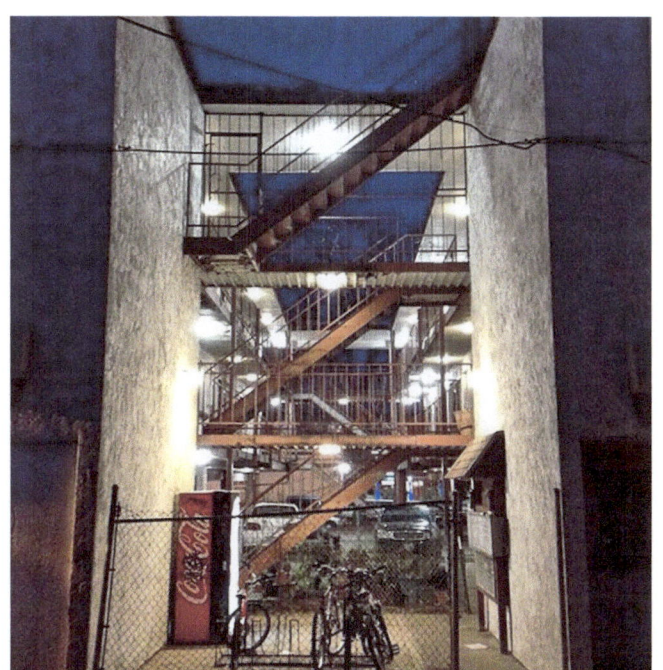

270 Lincoln

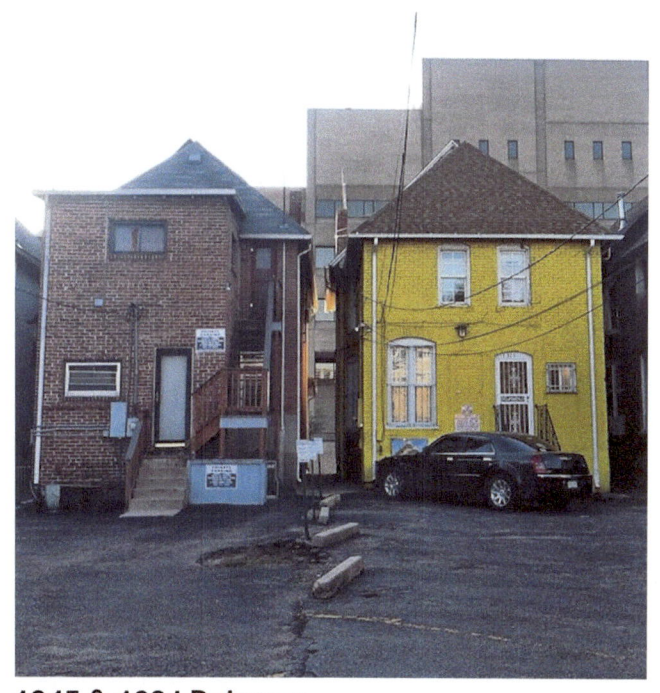

1315 & 1321 Delaware

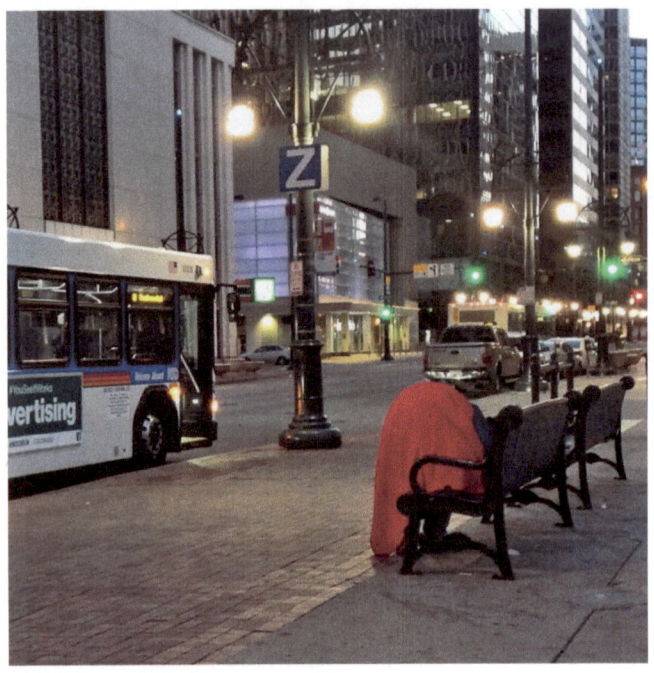

17th & California

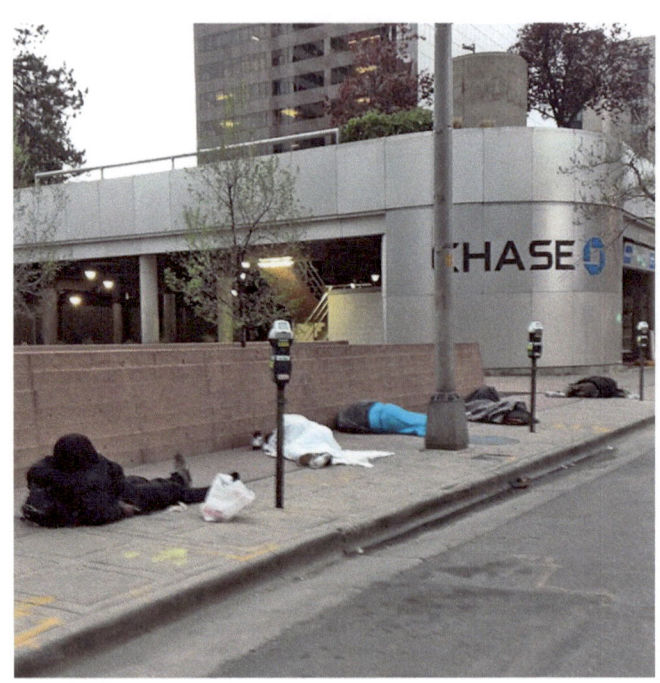

18th & Arapahoe

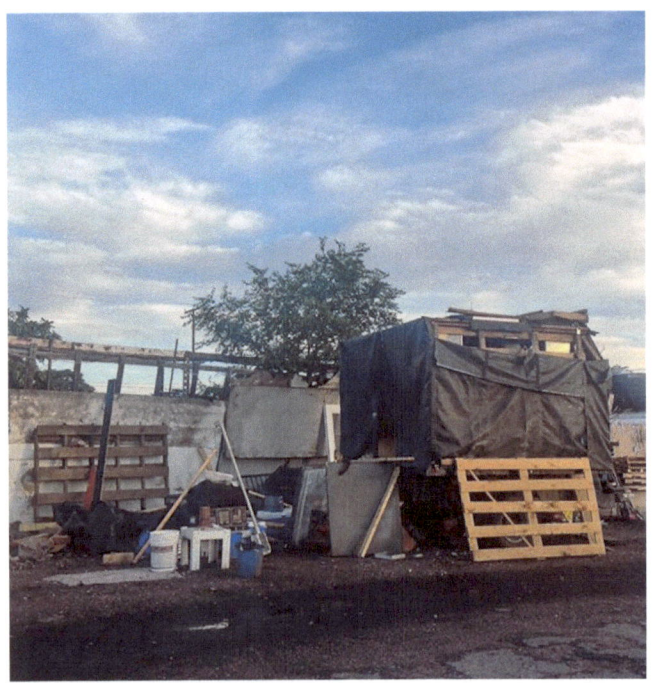

Hooverville off Brighton Blvd between 35th & 38th

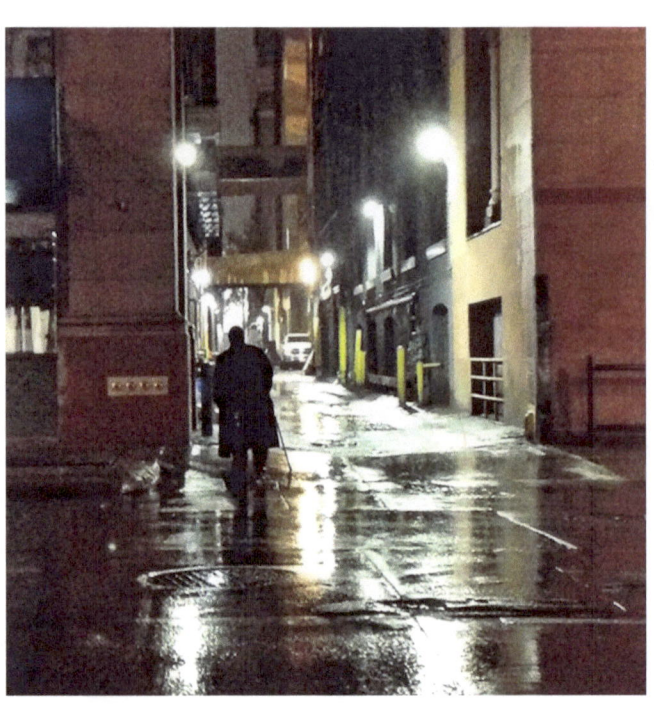

Alley off 17th between Stout and Champa

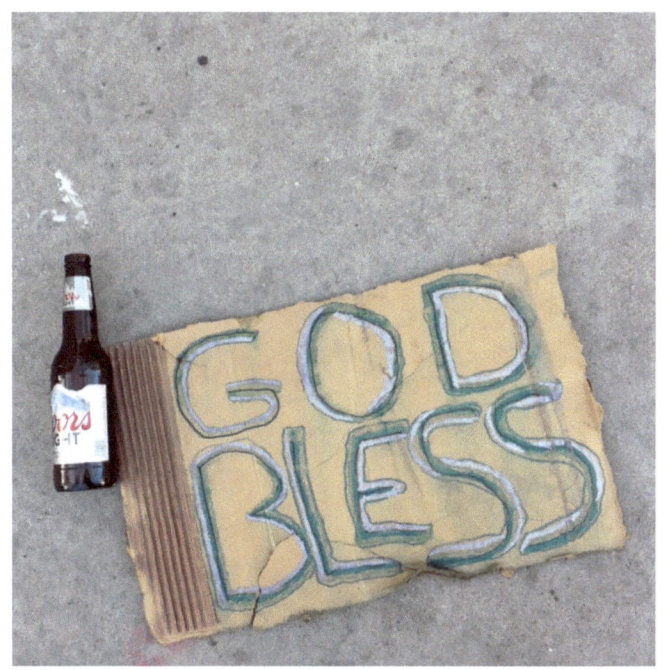

Wazee Street parking lot

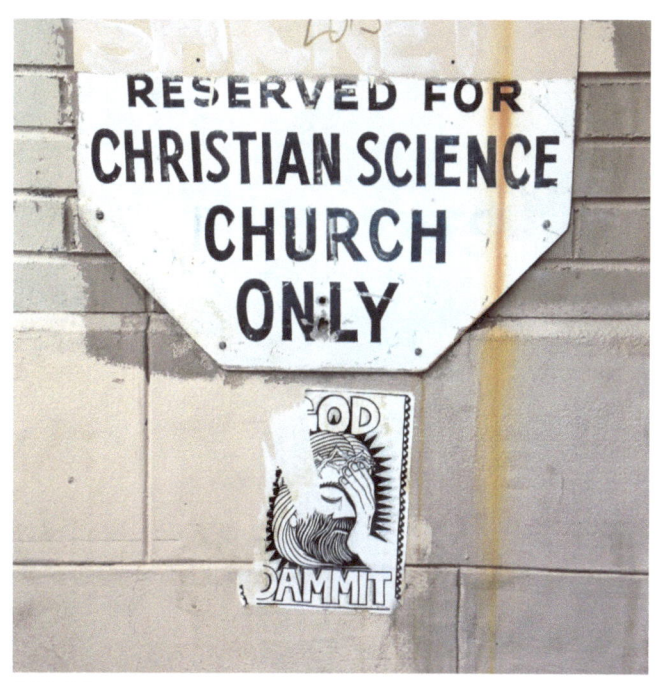

1401 Logan

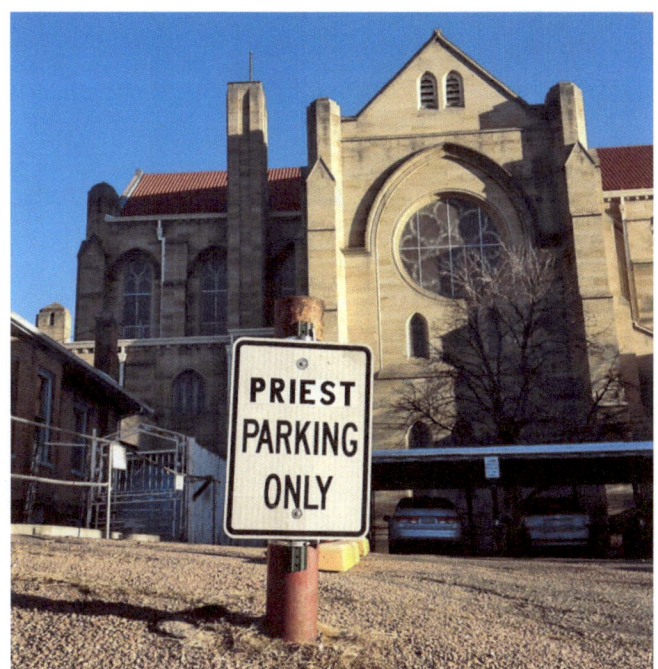

3005 West 29th

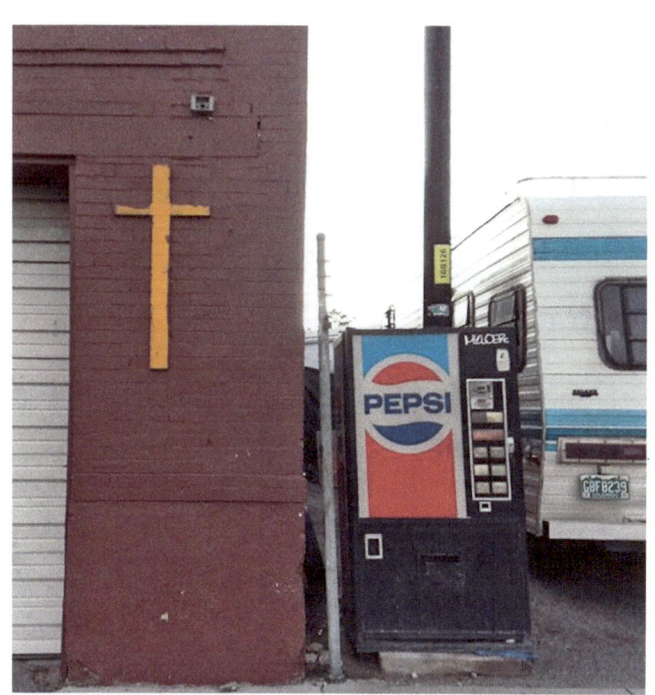

3632 North Downing

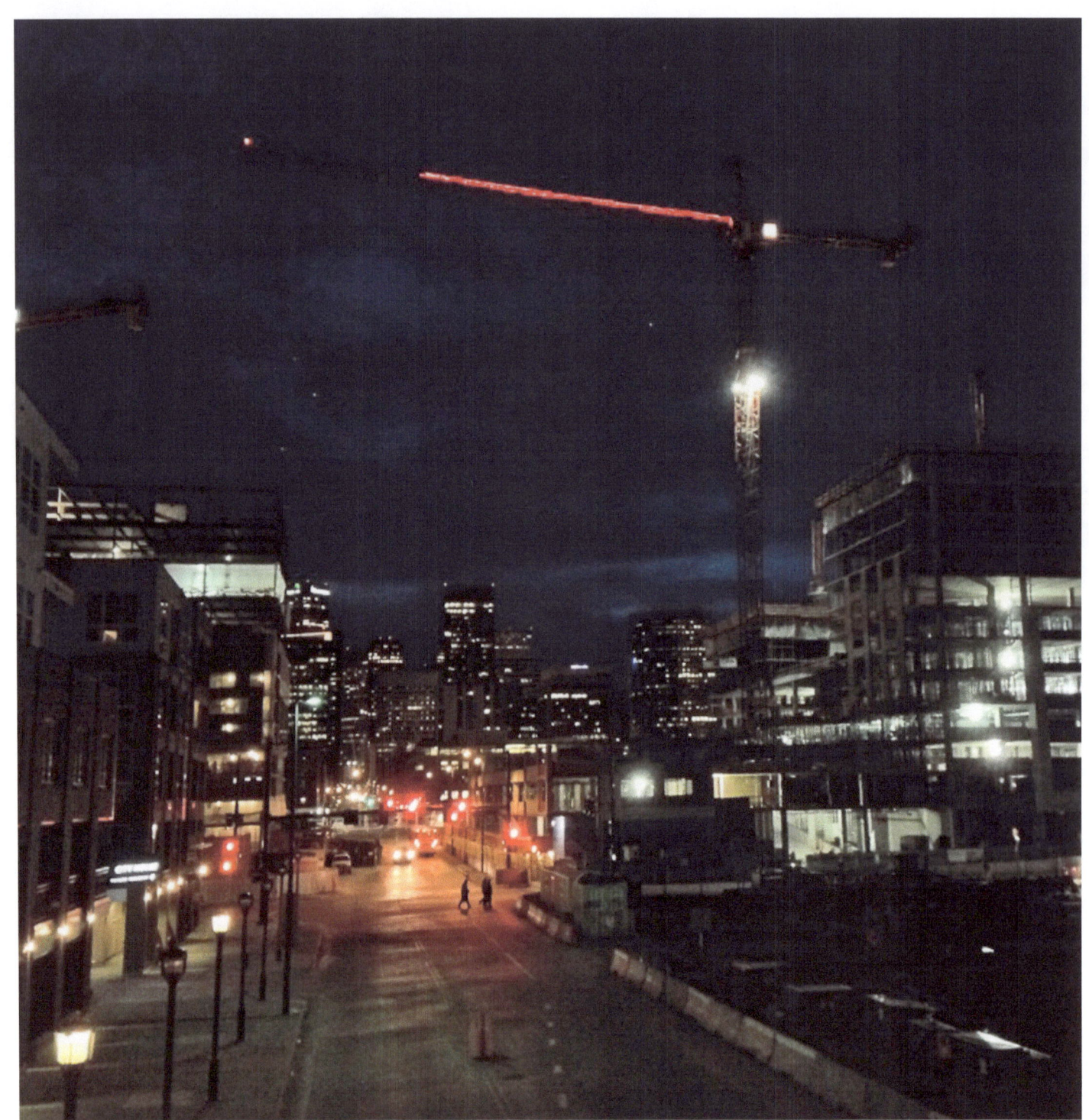

18th Street footbridge facing Chesnut

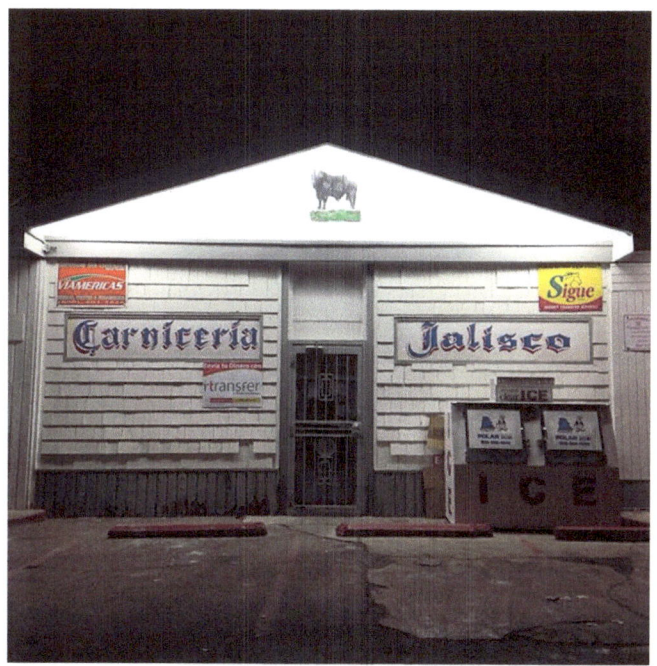

3300 North Downing

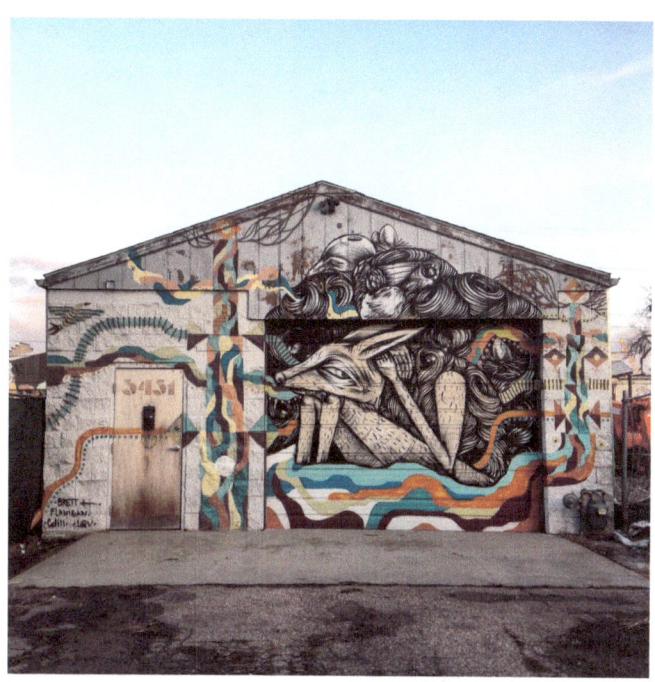

3451 Larimer

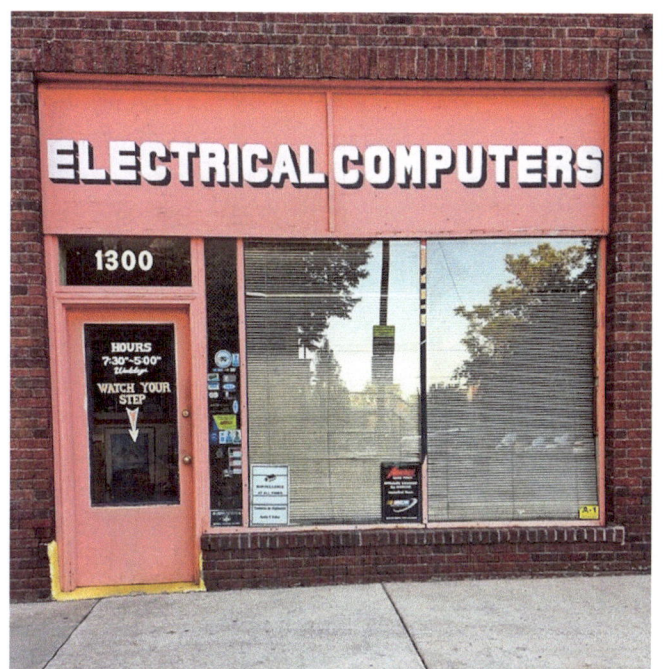

1300 North Ogden

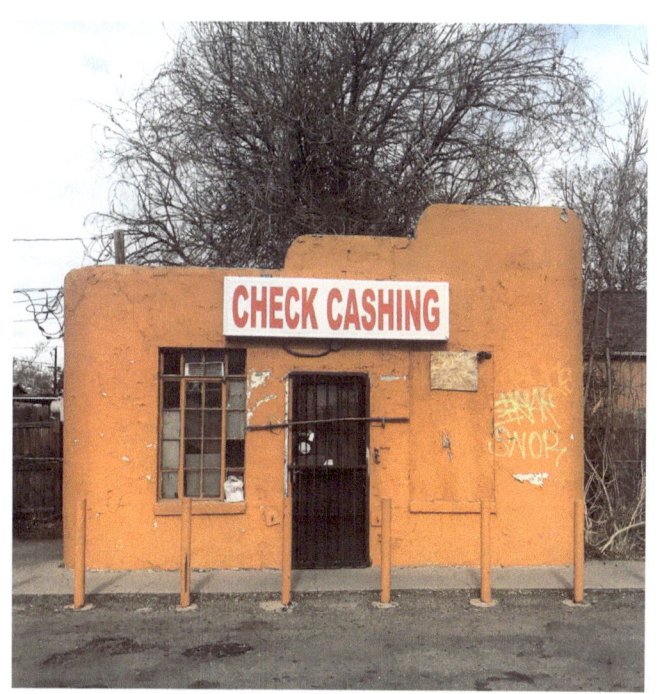

Somewhere in Elyria-Swansea

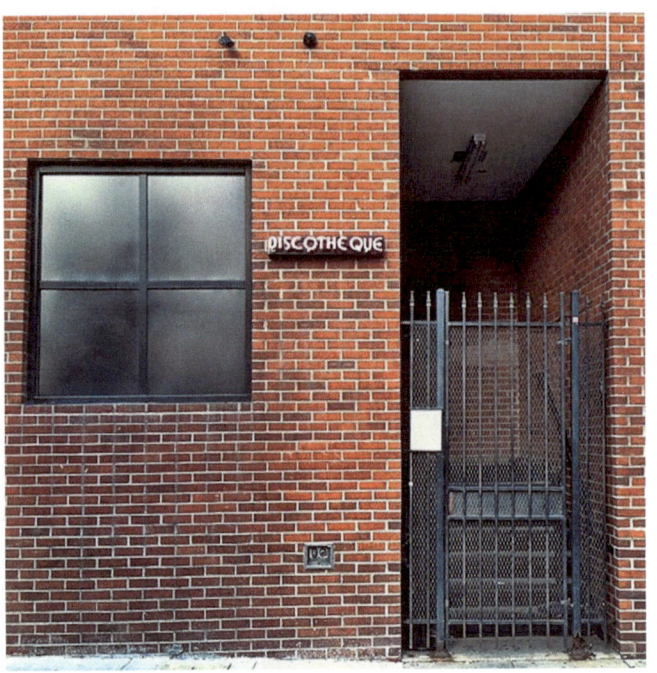
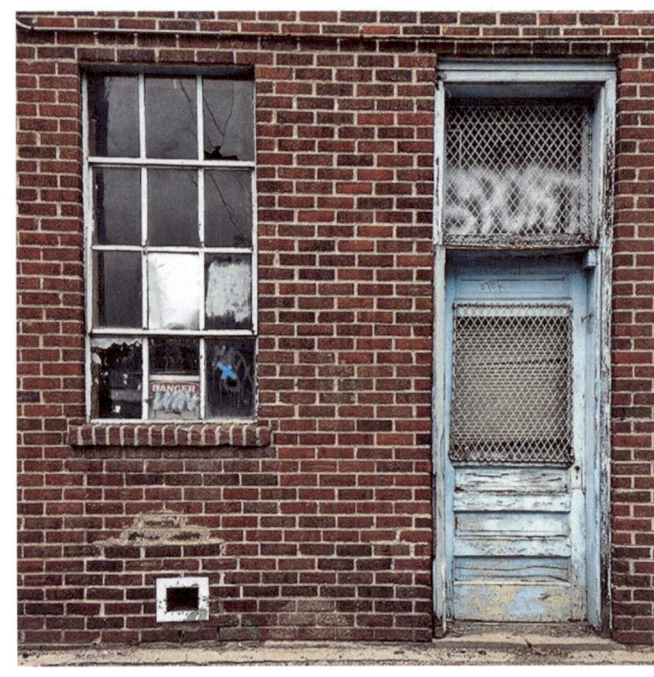
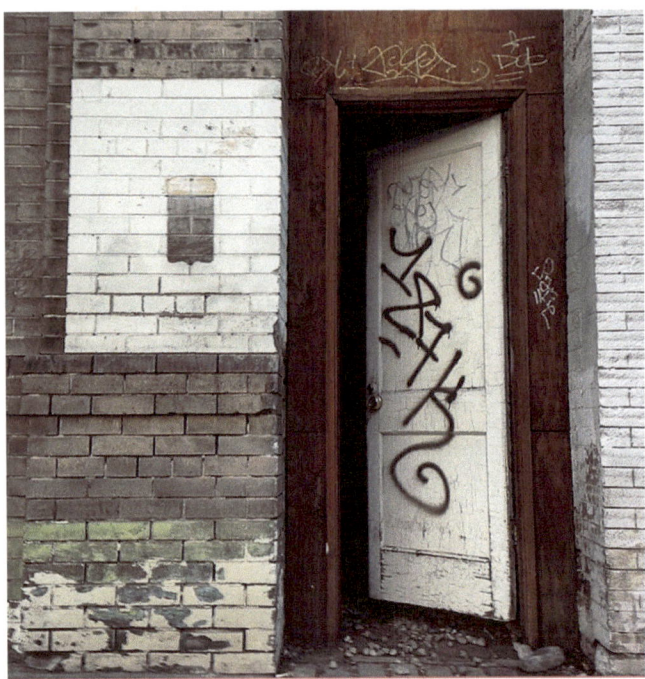
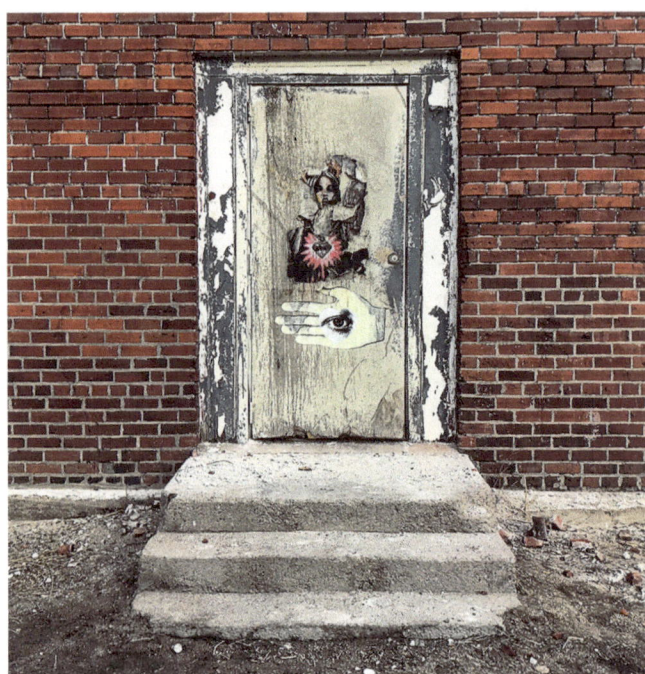

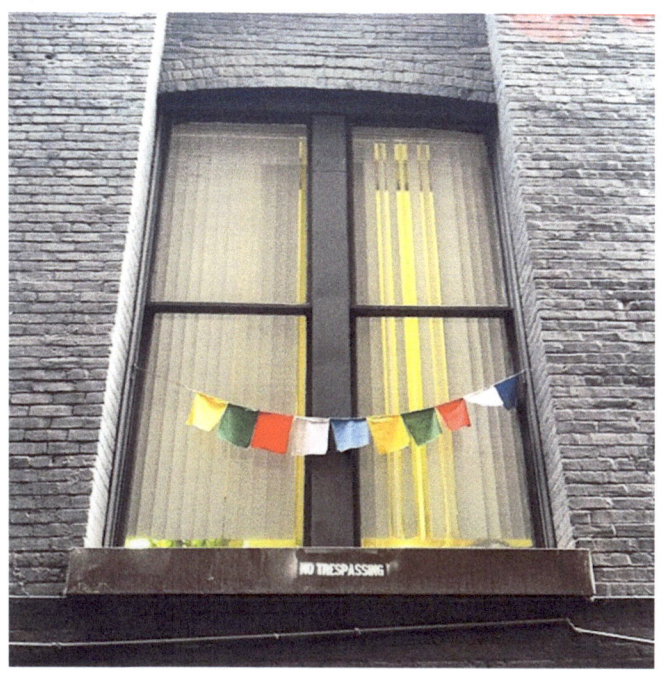
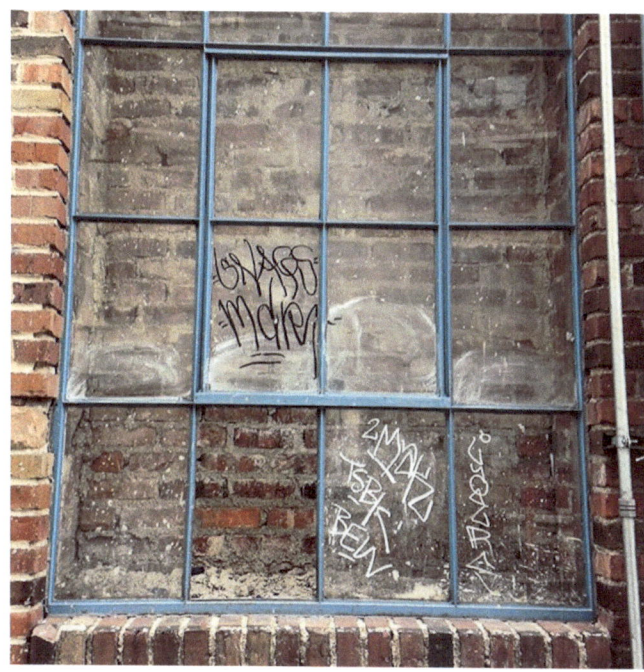
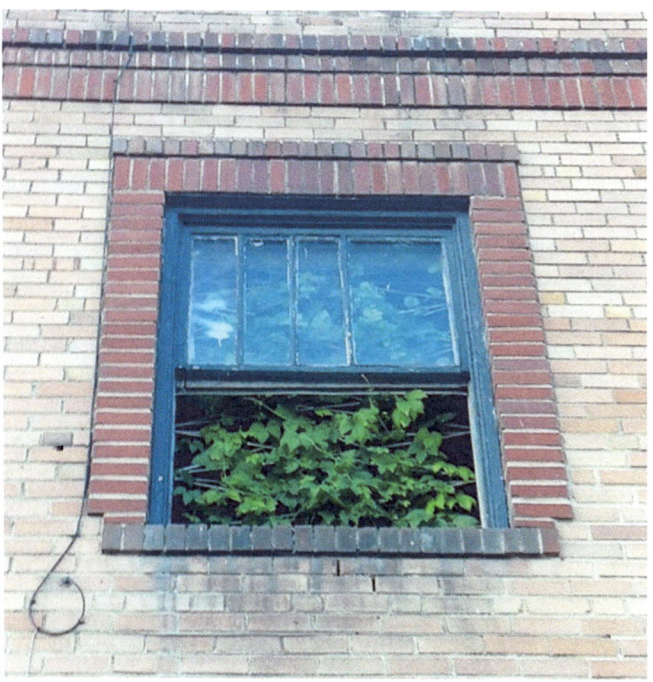
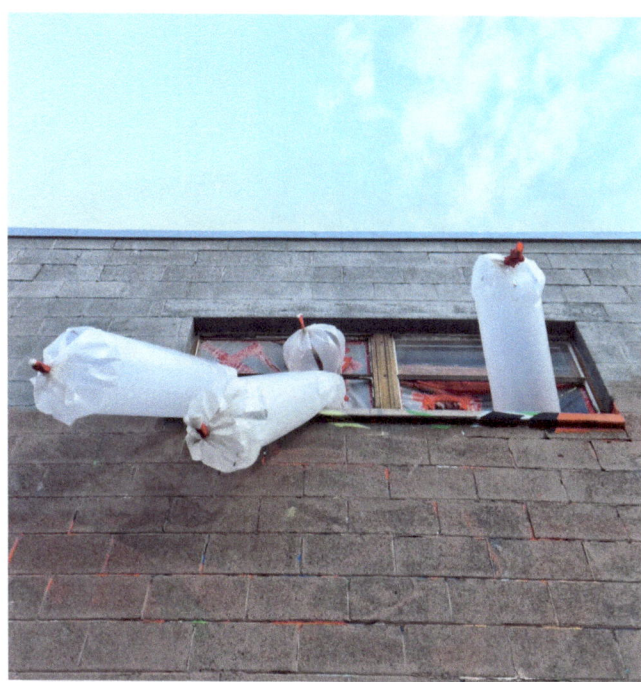

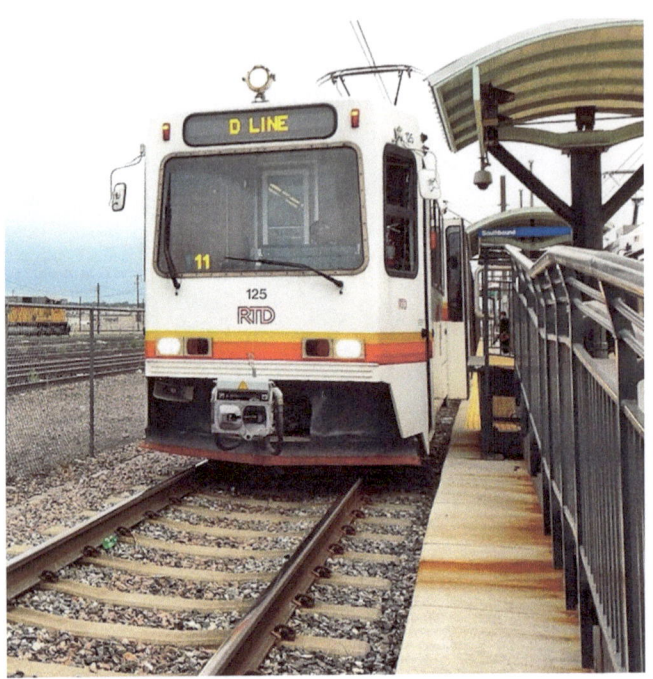

455 South Cherokee

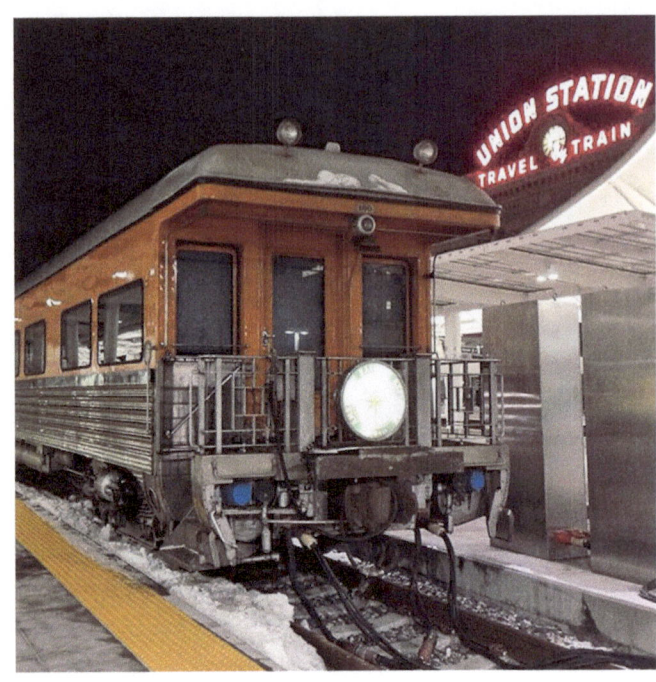

Union Station

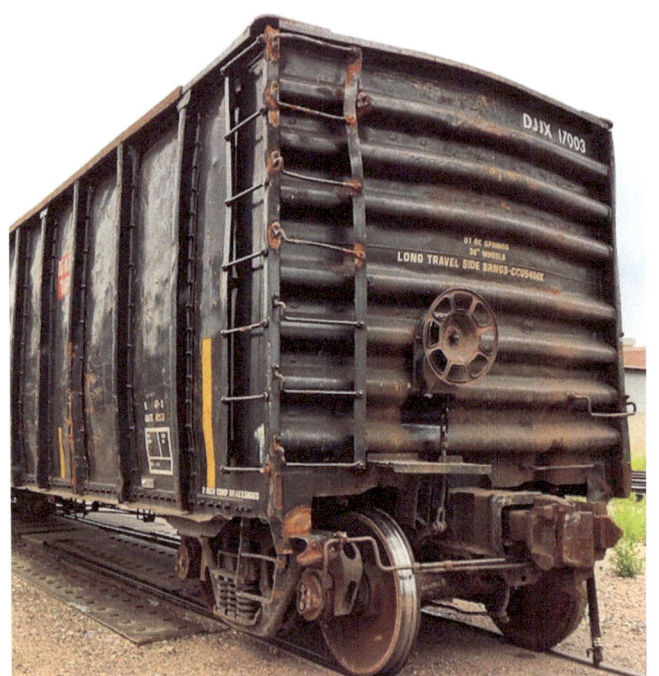

Globeville Road

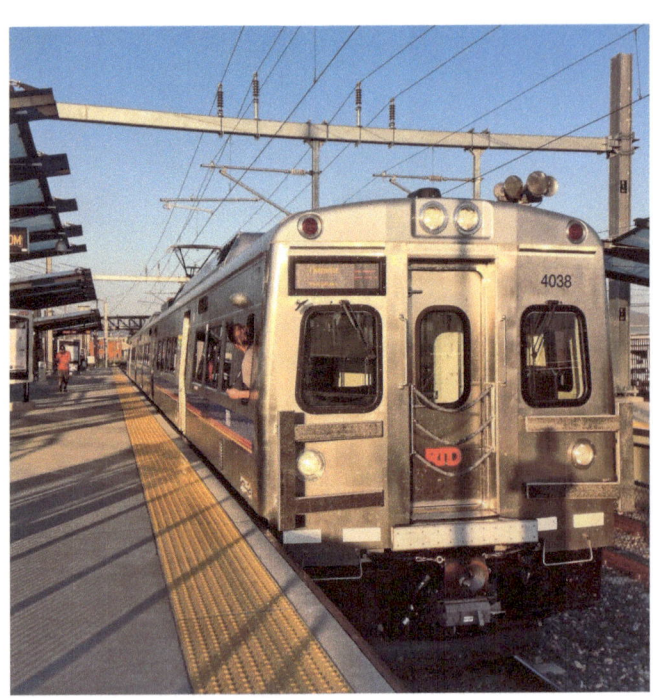

38th & Blake Station

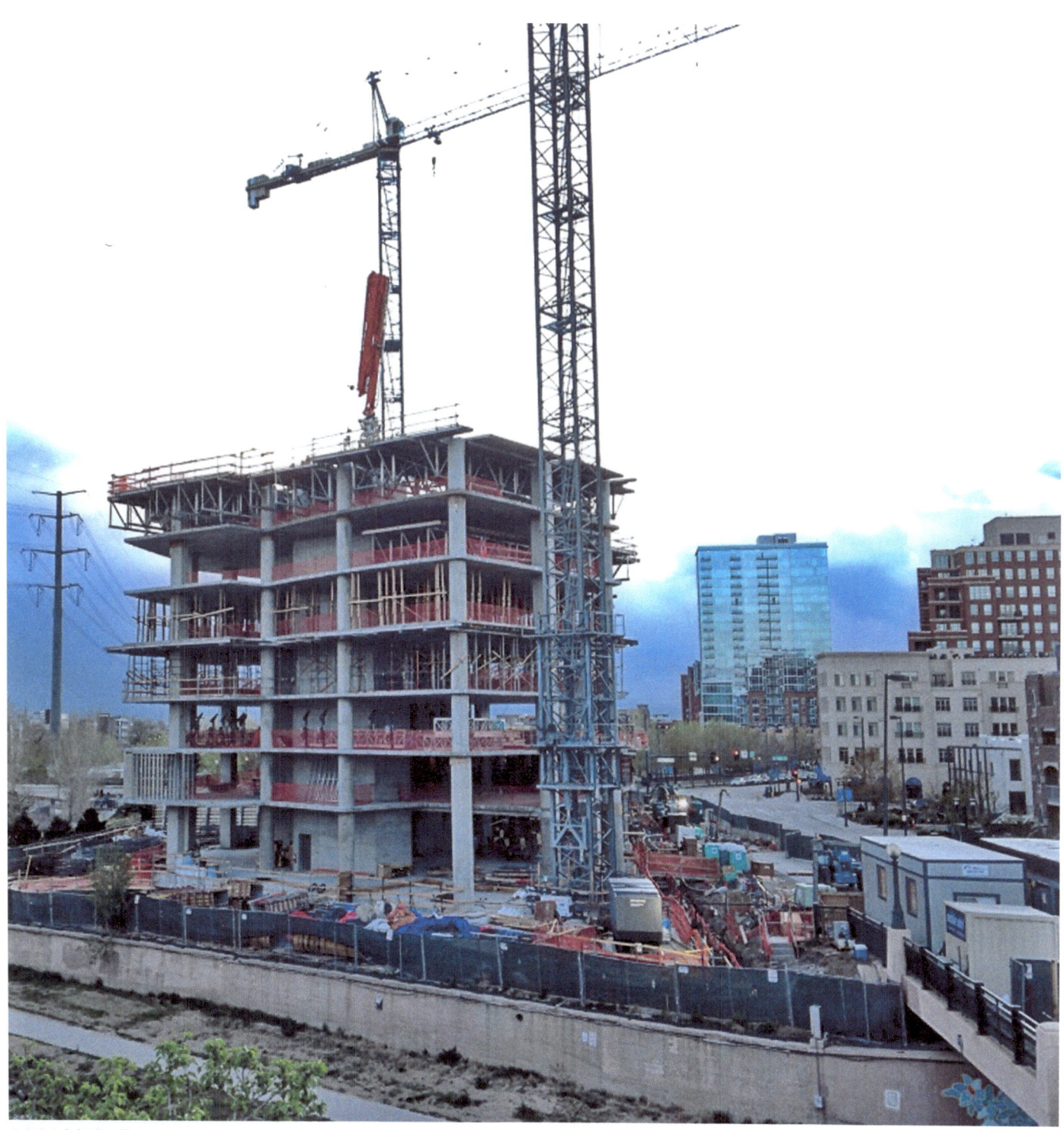

1441 Little Raven

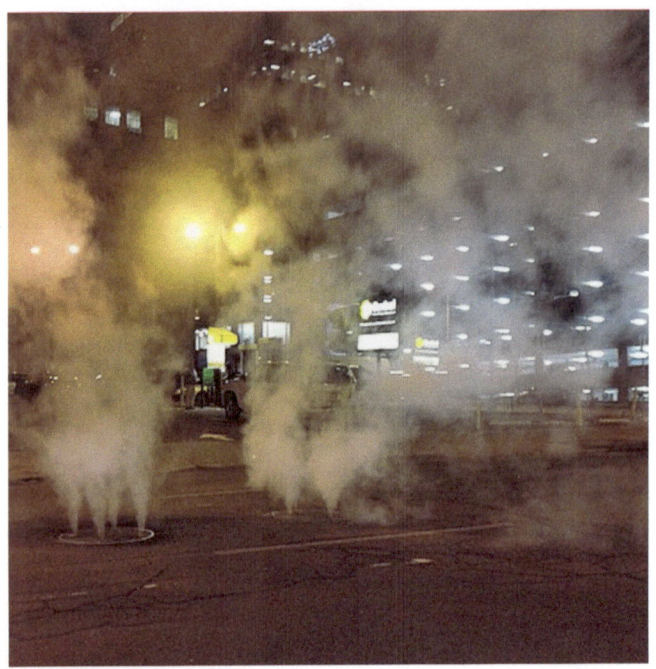

18th & Glenarm

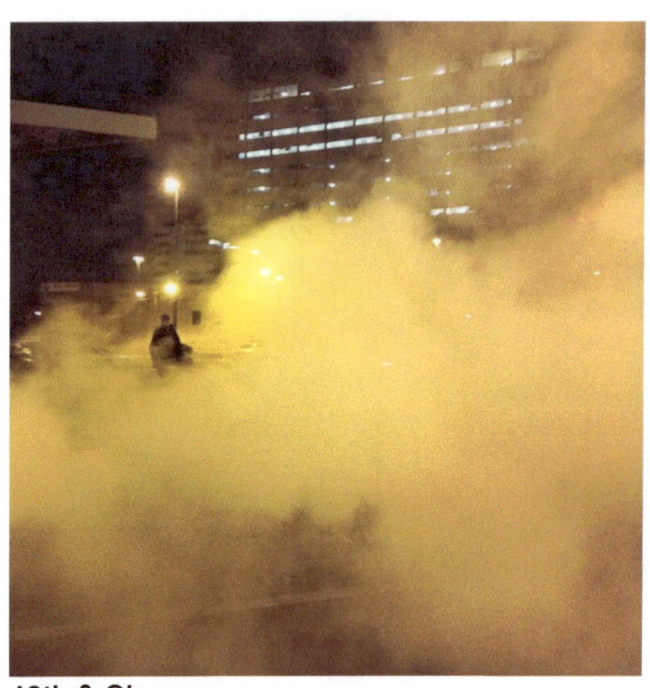

18th & Glenarm

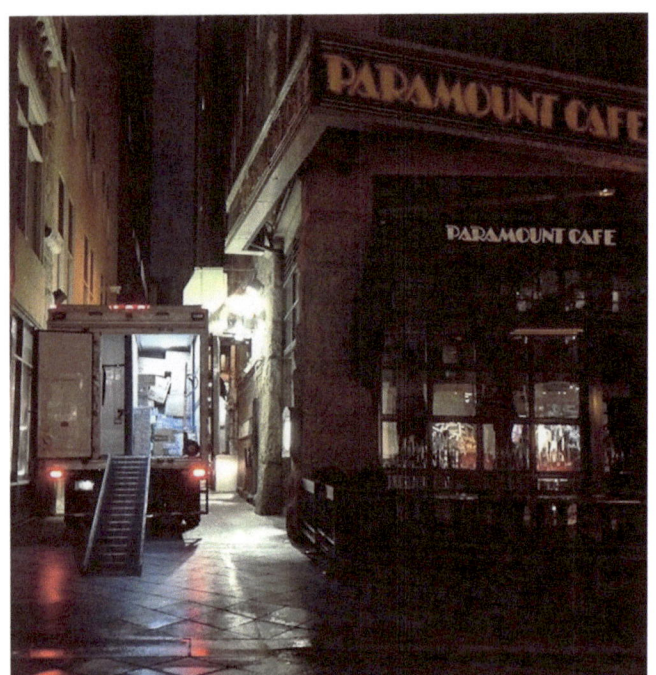

16th Street Mall

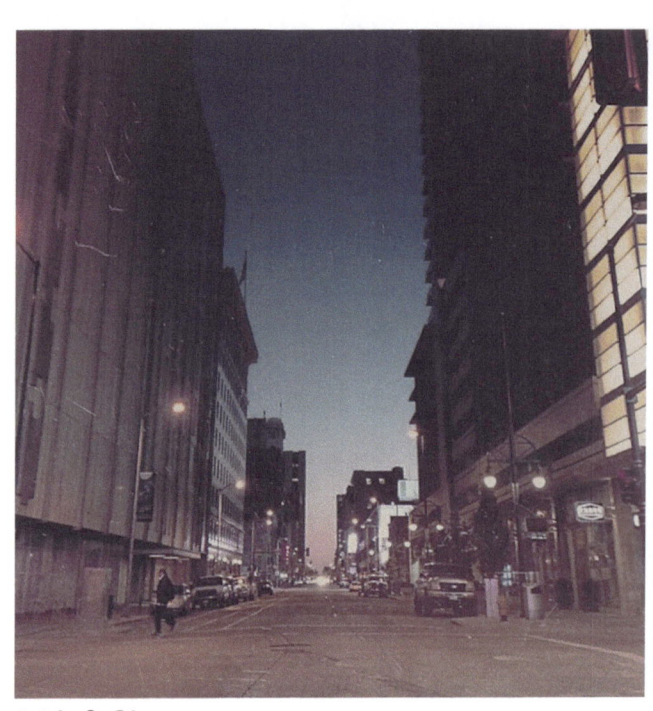

14th & Champa

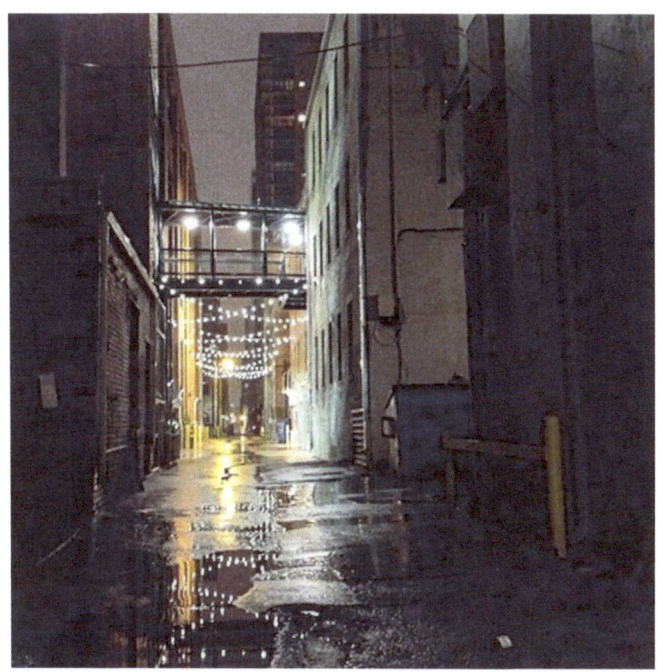

14th between Market & Larimer

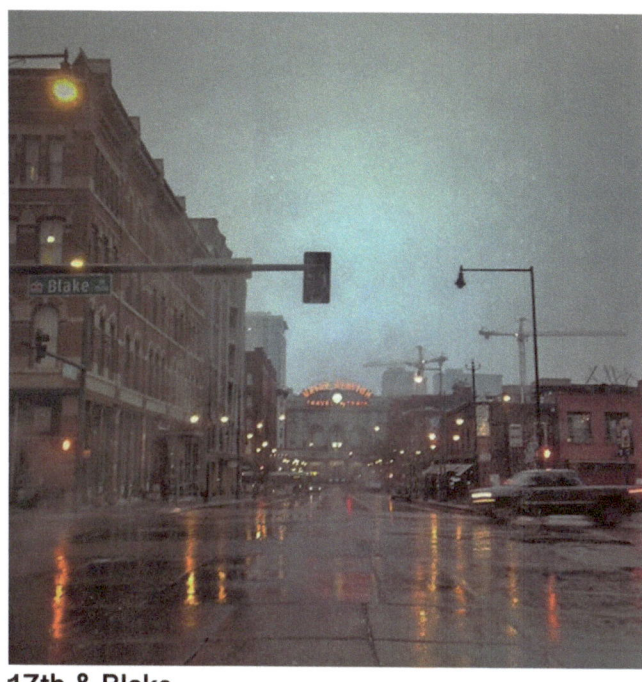

17th & Blake

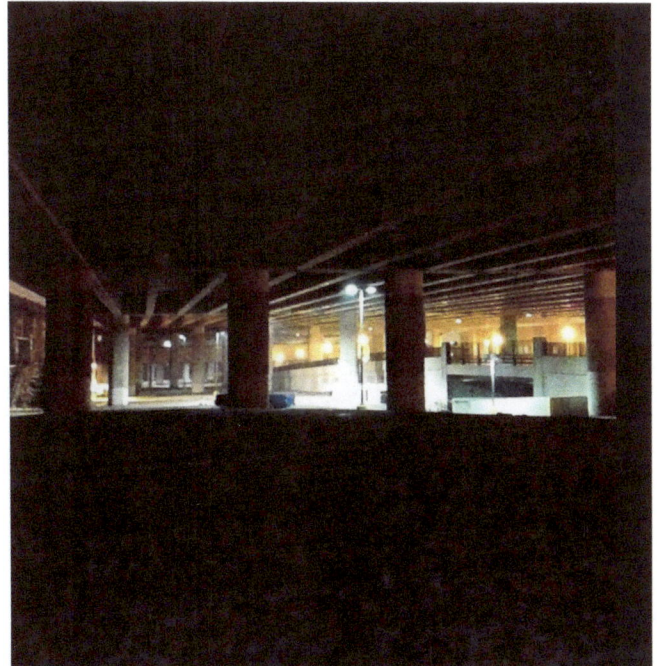

Under I-70 between East 46th Ave &York

Denver at dawn

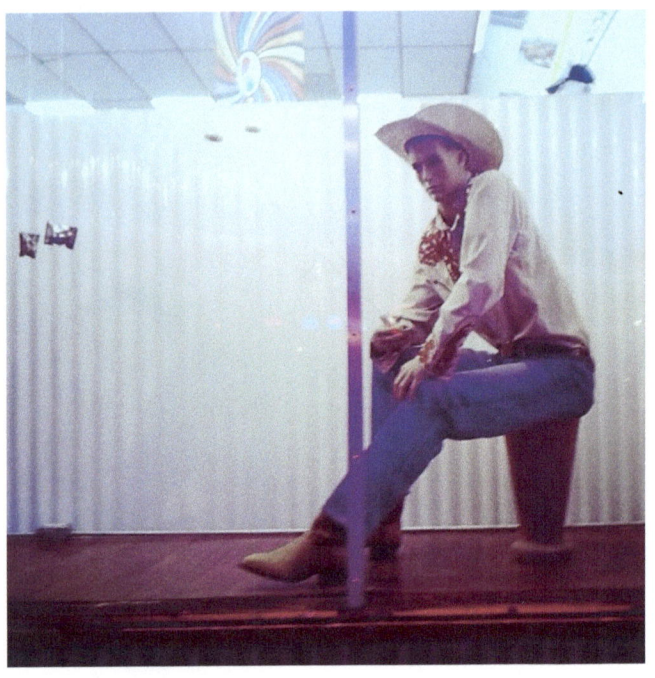

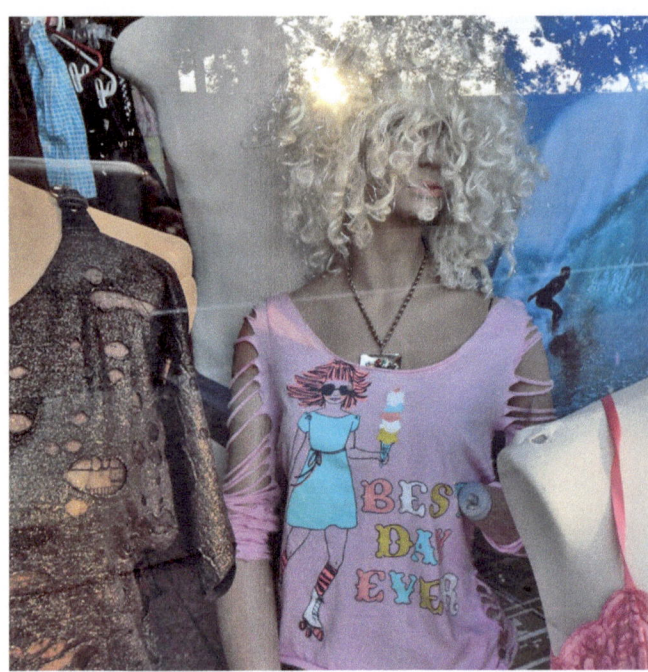

As my time in the bagel game was winding down, I had accepted a new position with a local up-and-coming restaurateur and she needed me 50 hours a week. I put in my two-week notice, then spent my last few days on the job training the next bagel delivery people, overloading them with maps and names.

On my last day on the job as the bagel delivery guy, I said my goodbyes to the staff. On my way out, I stopped to talk to our baker one last time. He told me a story about a previous delivery person, someone from "about a decade ago," he said.

He said that this guy was a nighttime photographer and carried his camera with him everywhere he went, taking shots inbetween deliveries just like I had. I could hardly believe my ears. He couldn't remember the guy's name but said he was now a well respected photographer.

I laughed at the sick irony of the whole thing and wondered why it took this guy three years to tell me this story as we high-fived and kicked open the back door to the alley for the last time.

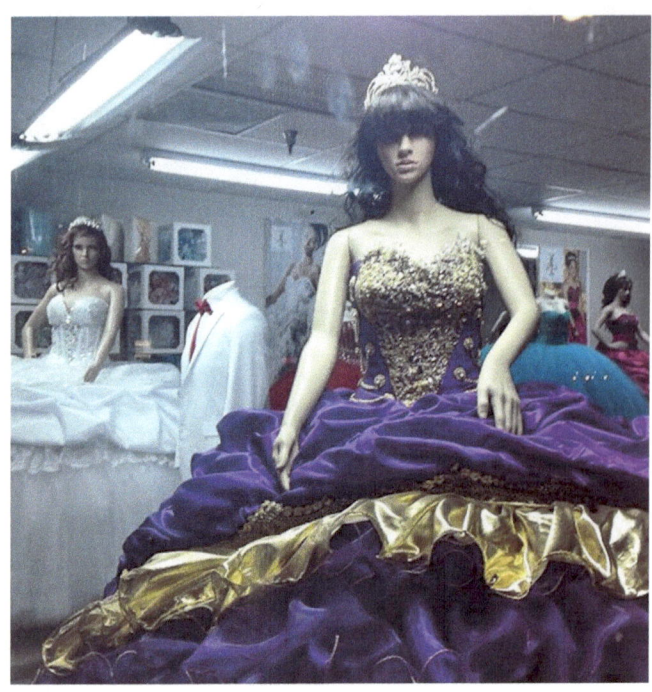

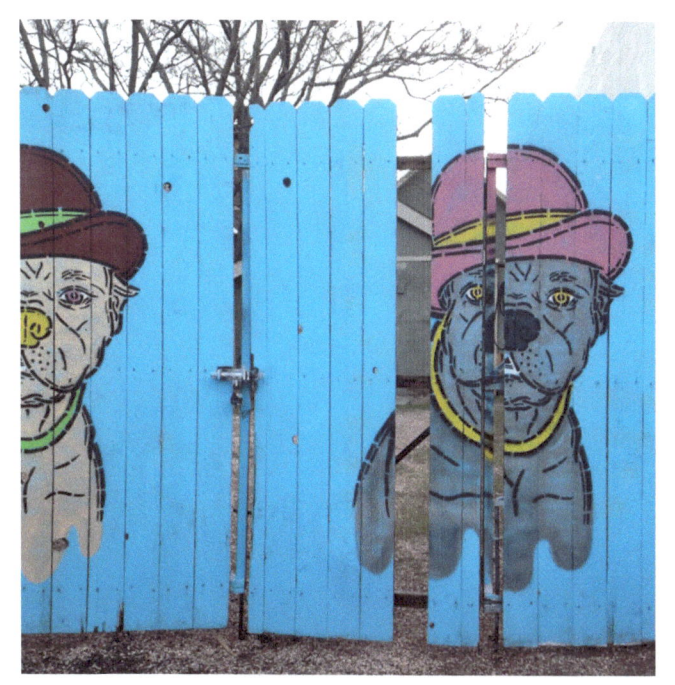
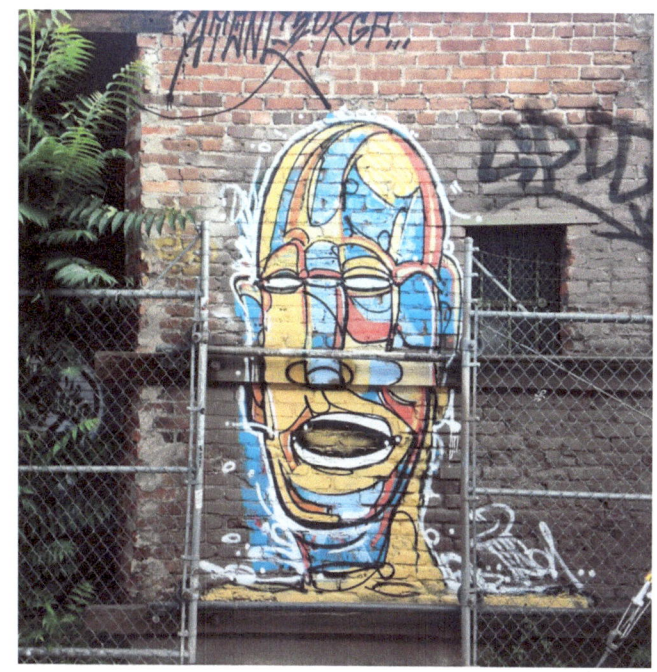
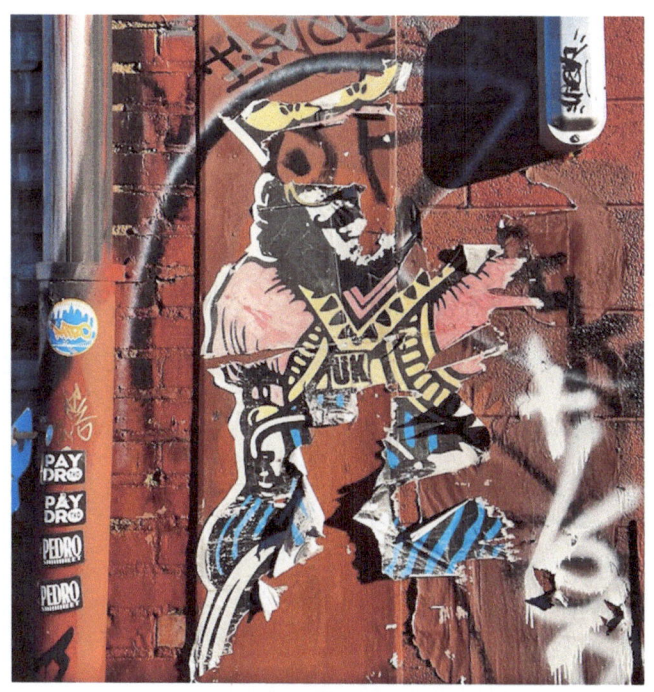
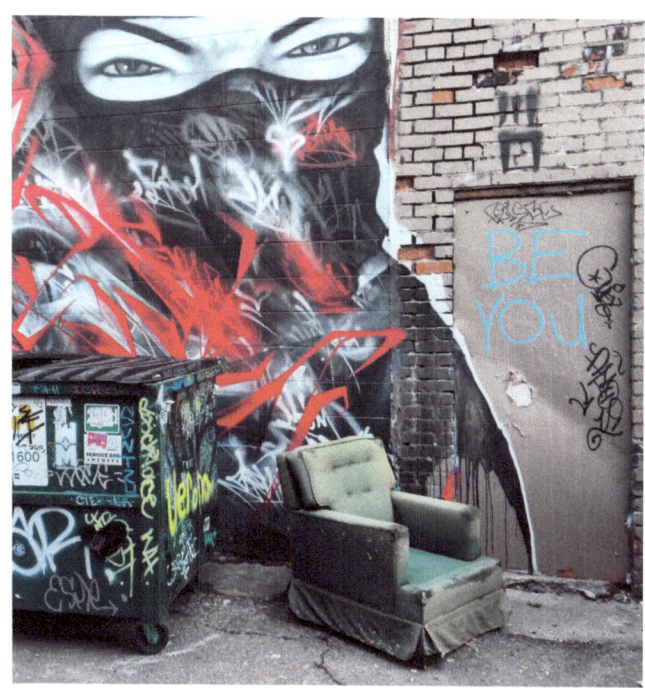

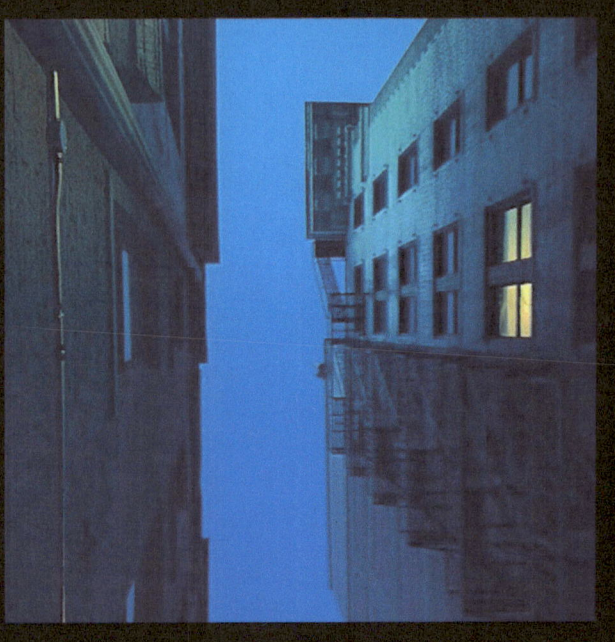
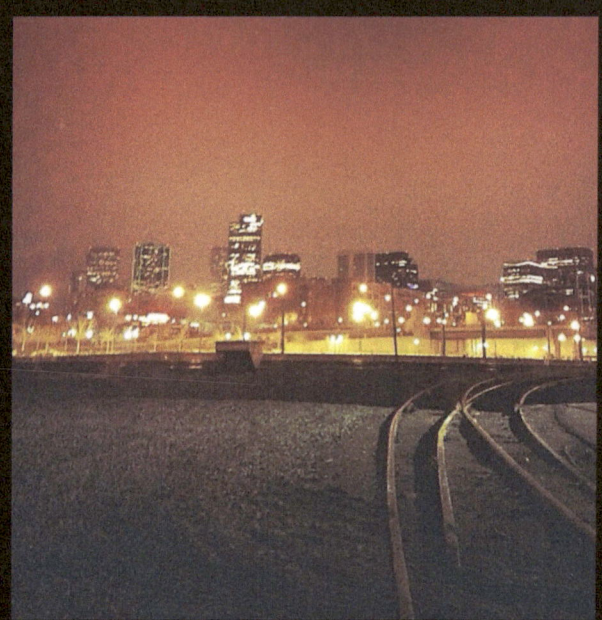
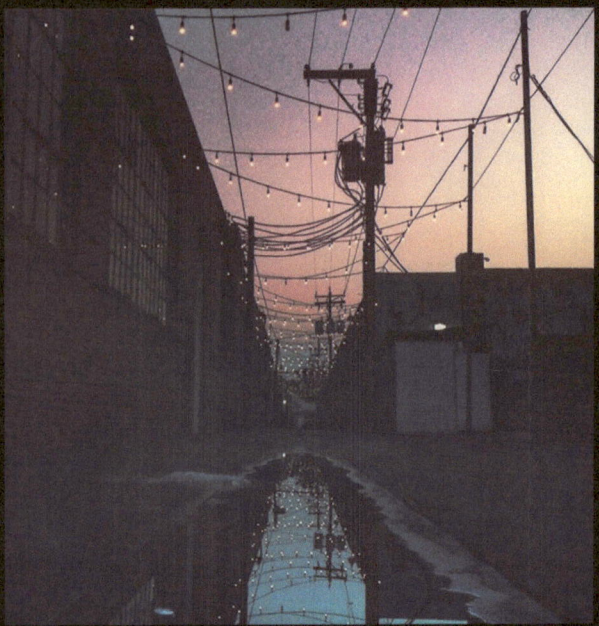
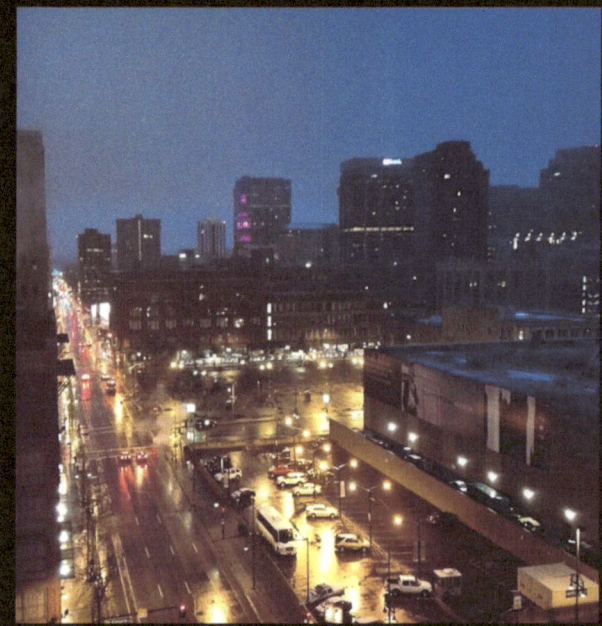